## KANSAS IN AUGUST

Patrick Gale was born an Aquarian on the Isle of Wight in 1962, whence he moved, via Wandsworth Prison, to Winchester. Here he served as a Quirister, then performed a lot and edited *The Wykehamist* before reading English at New College, Oxford. He lives in London and sings with the London Philharmonic Choir. Other novels include *The Aerodynamics of Pork* and *Ease*. Another novel and a study of Angels are in preparation.

'I'm as corny as Kansas in August,
High as a flag on the Fourth of July.
If you'll excuse
An expression I use:
I'm in love with a wonderful guy!'

[*from South Pacific:*
*Oscar Hammerstein II*]

Patrick Gale

# KANSAS IN AUGUST

ARENA

For Catharine
with much love

An Arena Book
Published by Arrow Books Limited
62-65 Chandos Place, London WC2N 4NW

An imprint of Century Hutchinson Limited

London   Melbourne   Sydney   Auckland
Johannesburg and agencies throughout
the world

First published in Great Britain by Century 1987
Arena edition 1988
© Patrick Gale 1987

'WONDERFUL GUY'
© 1949 Richard Rodgers and Oscar Hammerstein II
Reproduced by permission of Williamson Music Ltd., London

'GETTING TO KNOW YOU'
© 1951 Richard Rodgers and Oscar Hammerstein II
Reproduced by permission of Williamson Music Ltd., London

Printed and bound in Great Britain by
The Guernsey Press Co Ltd
Guernsey, C.I.

ISBN 0 09 954450 4

# Chapter One

'Who is it?'

Henry had just woken to thin sunlight and the sound of someone knocking on her surgery door. The knocking continued, almost out of control.

'Yes?' shouted Henry. The knocking stopped. A woman's voice answered.

'Room service.' The voice had a Canadian twang which Henry thought she recognized. 'I have your breakfast here.'

'*What*?' Henry clutched a sheet to her chin and sat up incredulous as the door opened and a young woman in pyjamas, dressing-gown and slippers tripped in. A perky smile was on her face and a tray, empty save for a urine sample, was borne carefully in her hands. 'Miss McGillis, you're not allowed up here without an appointment.'

'There we are,' said Miss McGillis, impervious. 'We thought you might not want to get up straight after all you've been through, so I fixed you up coffee, orange juice, waffles and a piece or two of French toast. How's that grab you?'

'Oh, that's just perfect,' said Henry, retching from the ammoniac smell. 'You can go now.'

'Be sure to have a nice day.'

'I'll try.' She waited until the door was closed, then lifted the tray and 'breakfast' on to the floor before reaching for the telephone. 'Doctor Metcalfe here, who's that? . . . Yes, isn't it early! Has your Miss McGillis gone missing? The Canadian? . . . Mmm. Well she should be nearing the bottom of my staircase now if you want to fetch her back where she belongs. Do try not to be so careless. She's been to the kitchen and might have done herself an injury . . . Not at all. Good morning.'

She replaced the receiver, then sank back on her pillow with a sigh. A gust of wind shook the open window on its sash cord and rattled the blinds by her desk. Pulling a hand from under the bedding, she picked the yellow bits from the corners of each eye and flicked them on to the lino. She focused on the alarm clock and swore. Bloody McGillis had woken her far too early. She rolled on to her side in an effort to fall asleep once more and came face to face with a pair of navy blue Y-fronts.

Somewhere in the building there stalked an underwearless doctor. Or was he a porter? That's right. A first-year zoology student moonlighting as a hospital porter to pay off his overdraft, and he was called Rodney. No, David. Geoff, possibly? Anyway, he had been terribly sweet. Henry had worked late on a report (still untyped) and had seen him over her eggs and chips in the canteen. His had been an unfamiliar face among the late-night desperados, so she had smiled in welcome and thereby drawn him to her table and her peculiarly seductive brand of conversation. He had told her of his girl-friend, Trish – Tina? – who was on a *kibbutz* being shot at by Arabs, and Henry had asked him back to a tot of whisky from her filing cabinet. Terribly sweet. And now sans Y-fronts.

It seemed she had barely drifted off to sleep again when the telephone rang.

'Henrietta?'

'Yes?'

'It's Candy.'

'Oh.'

'Candy. Remember?'

'Hello, Candy. How are you?'

'Fine. Are you awake?'

'Yes.'

'Good. You weren't at home last night, so I assumed you were working late on something. I've just got in. Do you want to meet me for breakfast? I'm not on till nine.'

'OK. Just let me have a bath.'

'Half an hour?'

'Lovely. See you there.'

Candy was an acquaintance from school who had resurfaced, without fair warning, as a psychiatric nurse with a husband and two children. Gently growling, Henry got up, wrapped her white coat about her and tottered along the chill tiled corridor to the nearest bathroom. The only good – well, one of the good – things about spending the night at work was the unlimited supply of extremely hot water that awaited one on waking.

She dressed in yesterday's slacks and one of the clean shirts she kept in the bottom drawer of her desk, gave her short hair a fierce brushing, made her bed and then sat at her desk with the navy blue Y-fronts on the blotter before her. Whistling through her teeth, she thumbed through the books on the shelf beside her and found the *Directory of Old Girls* from Saint Catherine's, Selmbury. This was dusky pink, with 'Henrietta Metcalfe' inscribed in a schoolma'amish hand on one corner of the cover. Under a bogus crest it read 'Lest We Forget' in Gothic print. Henry flicked through it in search of a suitably hated name, then addressed a large brown envelope to one Unity Pope in a house called Little Spark in a suburb of Newbury. She slid the Y-fronts, lovingly folded, inside and left the sealed package in her post tray.

Ensconced in the steamiest corner of the canteeen for warmth, she attacked a full cooked breakfast while Candy, who had naturally curly hair and the sort of disposition most kindly described as sunny, toyed with a cup of tea and a round of dry toast.

'But how are you *really*?' asked Candy. 'Are you still happy?'

'Yes,' said Henry, 'I suppose so. Reasonably.'

'I don't know how you manage. I was saying to Derek only the other day that if he wasn't there and all I had was my work, I'd go mad.'

'Yes,' said Henry, smiling at the forbidden epithet and stabbing a badly grilled tomato.

'But there's nobody *special* at the moment?'

'No. You know me,' said Henry, reflecting that Candy didn't know the half of her. They had barely known each other at school – Candy having been the 'Outdoor Type' – but Candy

3

seemed to feel that their shared education constituted suffi-
cient common ground for a friendship.

'How's that brother of yours?' asked Candy.

'Hilary?'

'Yes. Is he still acting?'

'Well, he's teaching at the moment. But I think he still wants
to be an actor.' Henry had told her all this last time they shared
breakfast. Candy had a short-term memory. 'He likes dancing
and singing,' she added.

'Oh, I *love* musicals!'

'I loathe them.'

'Does he look like you?'

'Apparently very. He's slightly less blond, though. He's the
spitting image of my mother,' said Henry and thought suddenly of a squeaky-clean grave beneath a palm tree. Damn Candy
for making her remember that.

'And how's your father?'

'Still in Paris.'

'It must be lovely to live there. Do you and Hilary visit him
often?'

'Once a year, usually. Hilary's too poor and I don't get off
for long enough.'

'Of course you don't.' There was a pause during which
Henry finished her second rasher of bacon and Candy crum-
bled her last crust of toast. Predictably it was Candy who was
the first to call out over the mounting clatter of plates and
conversation. 'I just don't know how you manage. I suppose if
you're a brainbox like you are, it makes it much easier to do
without . . . well, things.'

'I'm not a "brainbox".'

'Yes you are. You're much brighter than me, anyway.'

'All right. I am.'

Candy laughed, reassured of the happy natural order of
things, and patted the nurse's cap atop her natural curls.

('You're so inane I could bite you,' thought Henry.)

As she excused herself for work and walked back along the
corridors of shuffling, pyjama-trapped patients and starchy-
trotting guardians, she pondered the question of friendship.
She considered it odd that she found the woman whom any
outside observer would assume to be one of her only friends,
so utterly abhorrent.

4

# Chapter Two

Something stopped. Rufus opened his eyes and saw that it was the rain. His half-gummed stare crawled from the unfamiliar basement window across the near-empty bed-sit to the reassuring contour of the left arm on which his waking head rested. He dragged a hand along the floorboards beside the mattress and brought it back, black with dust, clutching a watch. Ten-thirty. The first lesson was at half-past twelve. Two hours to get home from wherever he was now, to change, grab some breakfast and his music case and get to . . . to . . . to wherever he had to be in two hours. Somewhere West. He let the watch fall to the sweat-creased sheet and tried to move his right arm, which had lost all feeling. Frowning with the effort, he raised his chin and swung his head to face the other way.

A girl – at least he assumed that that was what she was – was lying on her stomach, trapping his arm. She held her hands at her thighs, her face full in the pillow. It looked as though she had died some hours ago in a narrow space and been carried, board-stiff, to this resting place. The only evidence that, if dead, she had died *in situ* were the sky-blue skid marks where her stained hair had been rubbed around on the pillow.

As he stared at his arm disappearing beneath her moon-white form, Rufus found dim memories of a girl in blue leathers with a Mohican hairstyle to match, leaning aggressively against a night-club bar, and of a death-defying ride on her motorbike. The hair was now crushed in an unkempt mat over one shaved side of her skull. He couldn't remember her face. He pulled gently on his arm, to no avail. She gave no sign of waking, so he pulled harder and freed himself. Still she lay, arms at her sides, face in the pillow.

He strapped his watch about his wrist and stood with a mute yawn and a shiver. The basement felt damp. He glanced about for his clothes. His boxer shorts – a Christmas present from Hilary – were hanging out from under the duvet. He tugged them on and, finding his tee-shirt, pulled on that. His jeans lay on the other side of the mattress, entwined with the blue leather biking gear which he now saw to be plastic. As he started towards them, something cracked and sent a jab of pain through one foot. He stumbled – cursing in whispers – against a clammy wall and gingerly raised the wounded limb to inspect the damage. A used syringe lay crushed on the floor. He picked a jagged piece of its plastic from his sole and hobbled on towards his jeans.

Minutes later, as he let himself out and limped through puddles to a bus-stop in what turned out to be Lambeth, he remembered that he had bought an unaffordable present for his lover's twenty-fifth birthday. Patting his jacket pockets, he realized he had left it behind with the Mohican squaw. She was comatose however, and the bus was here and he had only two hours to get to wherever.

'Oxford Street, please,' he said and imagined his azure-topped hostess's doped dismay when she found he had left her a first edition of *Private Lives*.


'Wherever', as he remembered by the time he was leaving home in Spanish Place, was an army camp in the semi-industrial wilderness which battened on the prone flesh of Western suburbia. Near-deserted car parks, scrawny cherry trees and serried ranks of whitewashed fifties bungalows. Beyond the residential sector, a second fence marked the perimeter of an inner high security area which remained a mystery to Rufus. Most of the bungalows and certainly the tattered Nissen huts seemed deserted. There were never any troops in evidence; only patrol guards and a sprinkling of officers, purposeful in jeeps.

Mrs Phillips greeted him as limply as ever. Her dark roots were showing to such an extent that the lock which she kept flicking off her eyes was coloured half and half. One cuff of her housecoat appeared to have been scraped over the butter-dish during breakfast. She locked the front door again.

'Coffee,' she said dully, stubbing out her cigarette.

'No,' he said, 'Thank you.'

'Tom's still away,' she replied. As she passed him on her way to the sitting room she let the fingers of one hand slowly brush his thigh. He moved so as to return the pressure faintly, causing her to turn in the doorway and reach up to kiss him. Doubtless she had dabbed on her husband's favourite scent on rising, but there was strong tea on her breath.

'No. Play to me first.'

'All right,' she said.

There was a silver-framed photograph of her husband's regiment over the piano and a cluster of vivid pink hyacinths grew in a bowl on a nearby table. The comfortable, sagging armchairs, a fine rug and a Davenport-ish desk spoke of a prosperous county past and complained of the drear bunga-loid present.

As she took her seat at the baby grand and found her music, a smile broke out briefly. Every week she played to him before she led him to the bed she had shared with her husband until his departure all those months ago. She selected the piece with care; different each week, invariably sad. He stood beside the piano, which needed tuning, and watched the nervous play of her lips and her sudden darts to turn a page. He suspected that this preliminary recital was the part she liked best; what she paid him for. Perhaps Tom, her husband, was deaf. Perhaps he was dead. Today it was a Beethoven slow movement. She was a far better pianist than Rufus; this was sad, because her talent was wasted, but funny, because she had never heard him play.

He had twice flunked suicide and once come close to being in love. The first attempt on his life was in his last year at a harsh grammar school in Liverpool. He had been knocked out of a prestigious television competition for young musicians, one round too early to have appeared on television, and his father had made him an appointment with an army careers officer. He had started to cut his wrists, but had forgotten to lock the bathroom door and so was messily, farcically inter-rupted. The second time was only a year ago. Having failed his teaching diploma at the Guildhall School of Music, he had retaken it in secret. When the news of a second failure came through he had let himself into Hilary's flat, climbed into bed and drained a bottle of valium. Hilary came back from an unexpected weekend with relations in France and thought nothing of finding his lover asleep. Stirring – the bottle had not been full – Rufus had listened to the inevitable Rodgers and Hammerstein record, watched him clear his desk and turn it into a dining-table, answered his jibes and chatter where necessary. After the terrible, weak blank of narcotic sleep, Hilary's warm domesticity and unquestioning affection had seemed unutterably lovely. That was the nearest Rufus had come to falling in love.

As Mrs Phillips neared the end he felt, as he did every week, the tide of panic and disgrace lapping at his chest and when she stood and walked unbuttoning to the bedroom, as she did every week, he rose and followed.

# Chapter Three

Hilary looked up from his marking. *The King and I* had just finished. Having poured out the last of the half-bottle of Scotch, he walked unsteadily across the room to change the record. *South Pacific* was the only one of the pile still unplayed this evening; he had saved his favourite until last. As the overture rang out, he tottered back to his desk, took a gulp of spirit and then fumbled for his red biro.

'Lady Macbeth is a wicked lady and this is why she has to go mad. She can't cope with the problems of trying to be Queen of Glasgow, and a good wife and not let anyone know what she feels like.'

'Too simple by half,' Hilary began to scribble in the margin of the child's exercise book. '*Why* is she wicked? You rush on too fast; her wickedness needs at least a paragraph to itself. The same goes for her "wifely" qualities (*was* she a mother? etc.) Beware of writing can't, don't, shan't etc. as these are both inelegant to read and unlikely to be accepted by the examiners. You cannot always write in the way that you speak. There is no "u" in problems.'

He read on, inflicting red ink lacerations with barely a frown. This was the twenty-fifth version of *What are the reasons, if any, for Lady Macbeth's insanity?* which he had read that day. 15B were short on originality, even when it came to making mistakes.

The gas-fire was hissing softly and the windows were cloudy with an evening's condensation. Above the fireplace there hung a large, framed photograph of Mary Martin dancing in an oversized sailor suit. This was mirrored by a long, narrow photograph of the finale ensemble from *A Chorus Line*. A handful of small parcels lay in a bed of unopened envelopes beside the telephone. A half-eaten Chinese takeaway for two lay beside the desk. Rufus was four hours late and Hilary had been drinking conscientiously for three of them.

The telephone rang. He glanced at his watch and saw that it had just gone midnight. Dad and Marie-Claude calling from Paris. He downed the last half-inch of whisky and turned up the volume of *There is Nothing Like a Dame* before lifting the receiver.

'Hello?'

''Appy birsday to you! 'Appy birsday to you! 'Appy birs . . .'

'Hang on, Marie-Claude. There are a lot of people. I'll just . . .' He turned down the volume and returned to the receiver. 'Hi.'

''Appy birsday, darling. Quarter of a century; *what* a big boy!'

'Yes. Thank you. Sweet.'

'I 'and you to your father.'

'OK.'

'*Au 'voir.*'

''Bye.'

'Happy birthday, Hil.'

'Thanks, Dad.'

'Did you get our parcel?'

'Yes. It's right here. I'll open it in a sec.'

'Good. Got a lot of people there?'

'Quite a lot, yes.'

'Henry?'

'No. I expect I'll hear from her tomorrow.'

'Ah.'

'How's everything with you?'

'Marvellous. Great. How about you? How's school?'

'OK. Bearing up. Looks as though I might be kept on for another year.'

'Oh, that's good. No more singing and dancing, then?'

'Well, no. It doesn't seem so. Not for the moment. Dad, you must go. This'll be costing . . .'

'Rubbish. It's good to talk to you. Marie-Claude says, when are you coming to stay again?'

10

'Soon. I promise. Maybe Easter.'

'What's that?'

'I said, maybe Easter.'

'Great. You do that.'

'Well look, thanks for ringing, Dad.'

'Not at all. Happy birthday. Here's M–C again.'

'Marie-Claude?'

''Appy birsday to Hil,' she sang once more and laughed.

'Thanks a lot, Marie-Claude. Sweet of you to ring. 'Bye.'

'*Au 'voir, chéri.* If the present's no good, they'll change it at 'Arrods.'

'Fine. 'Bye.'

Hilary replaced the receiver. He fiddled with the dial for a few seconds then, failing to tuck the receiver under his chin, dialled a London number. It rang nearly twenty times before a woman's voice answered, faintly. He started apologetically.

'Hello? . . . Oh, look, I'm terribly sorry to wake you . . . I didn't? Oh good . . . Yes, I wonder, is Rufus Barbour there, please? . . . Thanks.' He waited while she went to look. Muted, Mary Martin was washing her man right out of her hair and sending him on his way. 'Hello? . . . Thanks a lot anyway. . . . No, no message. Thanks. 'Bye.'

Hilary raised himself back onto his feet and sauntered back to the desk. Leaning over the chair, he took up the red biro once more and scribbled at the foot of the last essay.

'23/50. Only fair. You have clearly read the play and grasped the gist of the story, but your essay lacks all argumentative thread. See me.' He flipped the exercise book shut and tossed it on top of the others in his briefcase. Then, turning the music up once more, he sat down to celebrate his quarter century.

He opened the cards first. Three of them turned out to be gift tokens from clinging aunts. There were several to 'Mr Metcalfe', bought by parents and grudgingly signed by pupils. There was one of Marlene Dietrich 'with loads of affec. and admiration from Brij xxx' and one of Vivien Leigh as Scarlett O'Hara from Richard, with a joke about 'never ever have a birthday again'. The last was from his sister, Henry – a funny card which he had seen before, with a 'P.S. Prezzy following soon'. Pat Casals, a fellow teacher, had bought him a nasty tie.

Marie-Claude also had sent him a nasty tie, presumably bought after careful browsing in the last 'Arrods sale. His father had given him a Rolex watch. This was generous; it was a beautiful one, remarkably similar to the beautiful Rolex watch he had sent the year before last. Rufus had sent nothing.

Rufus Barbour, twenty-seven, undiscovered concert pianist never in at midnight. He taught the piano at Hilary's school one day a week. A year and a half of undying love and half-hearted hunting for two-bedroom flats. Alternatively, eighteen months of climactic rows and botched reconciliations, or nearly two years of misplaced gratitude and sweet insecurity. Hilary sat staring at the gas-fire, feeling his jersey overheat and twisting the nasty ties around the Rolex box. Suddenly he fairly jumped to his feet. Lights, music and fire were extinguished in seconds and soon he was scarved and coated and out on the street. If Rufus had sent nothing, and wasn't in his flat, then naturally he was on his way to deliver his present in person. Despising himself for being so mistrustful, Hilary pulled the door shut.

He lived in a cramped flat over the Shiva Late-Nite Deli on North Pole Road. The school where he taught and Wormwood Scrubbs prison were within four minutes' bicycle ride. The street was aptly named, for the area had a feeling of extremity about it; the combined effects of lying beyond the Westway, being dissected by heavy twenty-four-hour traffic that was always hurrying somewhere else, and being surrounded by wide open but peculiarly lifeless spaces like the greater and lesser Scrubbs and the Latimer School playing fields. Directed simply to 'the North Pole', most taxi drivers knew exactly where to go. Just as Hilary had taken on a temporary teaching post while masterminding his career as the new Fred Astaire and had stayed three years, so had taken emergency lodgings over the Sharmas' shop and had proceeded to put down roots there.

He walked along the treeless reaches of Wood Lane. The wind was so cold that it burned his lips and it was beginning to snow. He waited in the shadow of the Westway for the lights to change. The flow of cars off the flyover was steady. There was a subway, but he never used it for fear of being mugged. He crossed the road and walked on towards White City station. Passing the subway entrance he fancied he heard a high-pitched wailing, like a baby's cry, coming from the dank tiled passage. He paused. The lights had changed, however, and the renewed roar of traffic deafened him. A snatch of car radio, perhaps.

On the wasteland to his left, where gypsies camped in summer, stood the Unigate Dairies building, a lone white citadel executed in a shade of Los Angeles cream. By the jaundiced glare of the street-lamps he could make out the fading Pepsi cans and dolls' arms which the wind had rolled through the sickly grass to come to rest against the chicken-wire barricade. To his right, the stadium was half demolished. Workmen had begun work last week, flattening the place with iron balls and bulldozers. One of the children had marched proudly into class bearing a yellow plastic 'W' which she had poached from the site on the previous night. Some of the old women in the post office had heard a rumour that a smart shopping precinct was to take its place, but most seemed less optimistic. Another patch of soulless nowhere; somewhere for people to throw broken radios. And dolls' limbs.

'When's the last West-bound train due in, please?'

'It says on the notice over there.'

'You don't know, off-hand?'

'We're not allowed to give out that brand of information in case we get it wrong. It says over there.' Impassive, the black woman waved a slow hand towards the entrance.

'Thanks,' said Hilary and went to look. The train was due in in five minutes. He walked about in the entrance, blowing on his hands. It was snowing in earnest now: large flakes flying, almost horizontal, on the wind. He read the posters, paced a bit more, saw a plaque he had never seen before which proclaimed the station a Festival of Britain prizewinner, and stopped to blow again on his chilled fingers.

There was a distant clatter and the train came in. As he heard the first footsteps on the stairs, Hilary prepared his face and wondered what to say. Were Rufus clutching a parcel or even an envelope and looking suitably crestfallen, he would be all smiles and would say something about having had a mound

13

of marking to do in any case. As the meagre crowd filed through the barrier, he stood well back. Rufus loathed public display.

Hilary tried to still his excitement. He thought back to Tuesday night. It would be like that again. Rufus would be drunk and sarcastic; having disgorged a cruelly inflated argument against their continued intimacy, he would vomit in the kitchen sink and fall sound asleep without brushing his teeth. There would certainly be no present. Oh no. No such token of even a passing affection.

There was no Rufus. An old man with a stick emerged from the stairwell and hobbled past the ticket collector, fingering his travel permit. Hilary stood a little longer, to watch the light go out in the ticket office and the ticket collector lock up her draughty booth, then turned out into the snow. As he overtook the old man and traced the chicken-wire back towards the flyover, he rehearsed the commonplace of his complaint.

Here walked he, good-looking – well, not bad – twenty-five – which isn't so very old, and certainly younger than some people – with a job that was only slightly soul-destroying and not unreasonably paid. Here walked he, who could do tap, soft-shoe, jazz, ballet (when he could fit in the classes) and sing like a . . . well, sing. Here he was, letting some failure of a pianist, who could only find a job teaching elementary classics one day a week, walk over his promising life. Rufus Barbour was a fully-qualified shit. Not only was he selfish and pig-headed, he was greedy, obstinate, morose, anti-social, parasitic and promiscuous. He delighted, as much as well-meaning friends, in dropping veiled references to his impulsive one-night-stands. What kind of mind is it that can't cope with steady affection, love indeed, but has to glean thrills from a succession of puny conquests? He was probably riddled with disease. Frankly, who wants to share their lover with half the trash and social misfits of Charing Cross?

Frankly, thought Hilary, as he kicked an adventurous doll's arm into the path of an oncoming lorry, I wouldn't half mind.

# Chapter Four

Henry came out from behind her desk to welcome Mrs Lewin.

'Mrs Lewin, what a surprise! Just when we thought you were doing so well.' She nodded to the porter. 'Thanks, Joe.' Joe left and Henry showed Mrs Lewin to the sofa. The corpulent visitor arranged herself on its edge and her night-dress over her knees. Henry sat in an upright chair beside her. She gave a wry smile. 'We found you a flat and a perfectly good job weeks ago – what went wrong?'

Her deskside manner was understanding without undue sympathy. She would nod slowly as she listened to an explanation. Her voice was gentle, low in pitch and only the faintest irony pulled at the edges of her smile. Her cheeks were high and smooth, but her forehead was heavily scarred through an habitual raising of the eyebrows.

Mrs Lewin had relaxed in Joe's absence and was now leaning a thick forearm on one knee so as to bring her nose closer to Dr Metcalfe's.

'Well, I suppose it was all OK; nice flat and that. Don't think I wasn't grateful. The work wasn't bad, it was just the people. They didn't . . .' She broke off, wheezing, to cough heavily and swallow what she produced. 'Pardon. No, the people there didn't understand, you see.'

'What didn't they understand?'

'The kids. They came back you see, like I said they would.'

'Were you still taking the medicine?'

'Well . . .'

'Now be honest. It's important.'

'Well, no. It wasn't doing any good.'

'How can you tell if you weren't taking it?'

'The kids came back, didn't they?'

'But was that before or after you stopped taking the pills?'

'Before. No after. No, it must've been before, because it was them as told me to stop taking the medication.'

There was a pause as Henry looked briefly at her hands, then she raised her gaze full on to Mrs Lewin's uncertain face. Very slightly she smiled.

'Are you sure?' Mrs Lewin looked away and twisted a piece of nightdress in her great, liver-spotted hands. 'Because I can never be quite sure if you're telling the truth.'

'It's not me, it's the kids as don't tell the truth.'

'Then why did you listen to them when they told you to stop taking the pills?'

'Well, you've got to listen to your kids, haven't you?'

'I couldn't say. How many came back?'

'Five.'

'Five? You're sure of that?'

'Yeah. Five,' answered Mrs Lewin, gleaning assurance from repetition. 'I counted them; Mandy, Louie, Della, Pete and Joey.'

'Joey? He's new.'

'Yeah, well Della died, didn't she?'

'But you just said that Della was one of the five.'

'I didn't mean Della, I meant Sam.'

'Before you left us last time, there were only four, and Della was never one of them.'

'Yeah, well she came and went pretty fast.'

'So it would appear.' Henry waited to see if there was any answer to that, but apparently there was none. 'What went wrong at work, then? You say the other people didn't understand?'

'That's right. I told them about the kids and they thought I was weird.'

'I thought we had come to an agreement on that. I've told you repeatedly that however real they seem to you, you can't expect other people to be interested.'

'You're interested.'

'That's my job. But they're not my children – they're yours and they're totally your responsibility. You know they only

16

come when you stop taking the pills, and you know that if you let them come and you start talking about them, people are going to think you're funny.'

'They said I was loony.'

'That's what people out there call people in here. You know that. It's not rude really; it's simply a way of saying, "We don't understand you because you're different." '

'Well, I think *they're* different.'

'Of course you do, and they are, but unfortunately there are more of them than you. You're the only woman I know with five children called Mandy, Louie, Della, Pete and Joey who live inside your tummy and come and go as they please.'

'Sam. Della's copped it.'

'Sorry, Sam. Is he there now?'

'Yeah. 'Course.'

'What is he doing?'

'I'll ask him.' Mrs Lewin cocked her head on one side so that a strand of lank, black hair fell over her eyes. She stared at the window. 'Sam?' she called. 'Sam? What are you doing now?' She waited and mouthed counting one to five before she answered, triumphantly, 'He says he's looking for meat and he can't find any.'

'Is that your way of saying you want your supper?'

'No. I'm not hungry, but Sam is, and Della.'

'I thought Della was . . .'

'I mean Louie,' Mrs Lewin corrected herself hastily. 'Louie's hungry too; they're all bleeding ravenous. Filthy lunch today. They didn't like that suet much.'

'Mrs Lewin?'

'Yeah?'

'Do you like it here?'

Mrs Lewin slipped her great hands coyly under her thighs like a seven-year-old faced with a cameraman and gave a girlish wiggle.

''Course I do,' she said. 'It's where my friends are.'

'Well, you're not going to be here for long. You're not what anyone could call "ill" any more. We'll just keep you here for a couple of weeks to get you back on your pills and while we find you another job and then the holiday's over. Is that clear?'

'Yes, doctor. Thanks ever so.'

17

Henry stood and held out a hand to help her out of the sofa.
'Come along then. Let's find you your supper. Just wait a
second while I collect my things.'

Mrs Lewin stood buttonning up her dressing-gown while
Henry pulled on an overcoat, threw a few papers and yesterday's shirt into her briefcase and switched off the desk-lamp.
Then she guided her patient back to her ward in search of
supper for the kids.


Dr Henrietta Metcalfe suffered from truncated youth. Born in
Kuala Lumpur, where her father had held a post in an oil
company, she was an only child for the first ten years of her
life. Her mother then died from various complications on
presenting her with a little brother by bungled Caesarian
section. Henrietta was promptly despatched to a suitably
protective English boarding school – the Saint Catherine's,
Selmbury, where she met Candy – while the family *amah* cared
for baby boy and grieving father. The oil company paid her air
fares, so she came home for every holiday and donned her
mother's apron. Through her teens she helped her father at
dinner parties and taught her brother to swim, sew and make
pastry. While her neighbours were playing badminton in the
joyless heat she would sit on the verandah to supervise Hilary's
reading of *Winnie the Pooh* and later, to instruct him in the
uses of his chemistry set. It was only in her twenties, when it
was too late not to forgive him, that she came to think of him
as a matricide.

Her memories of her mother were more sensuous than
historic; a deep, amused voice, still warm empty sheets, arms
hard from squash, a hesitant piano rendition of 'Can't Help
Lovin' That Man' and rose geranium bath oil. Hilary had
inherited her permanently tousled, dirty blonde hair along
with most of her features, so that the mere sight of him could
set unshed tears burning in her stomach. Thanks to the
censorship of a merciful mind, she could remember no grieving. Her father claimed that she had not spoken for a week.

'Right you are, Dr Metcalfe.'

'Thanks.'

The gatekeeper swung up the barrier and Henry drove out

of the hospital compound in her battered yellow Spitfire. In the lane leading to the motorway she had to mount the pavement in order to outmanoeuvre a broad brown puddle on which floated balls of rotting paper, dead leaves and the remains of a sizable animal. The services strike had lasted two months now. Apparently the transport people had returned to work, for she had seen buses around Hammersmith, and there were fewer hitch-hikers than before. Incinerator skips were still stationed, smoking, at regular intervals. Luckily the hospital had a series of cess-pits as well as a furnace, so nurses' fears about the installation of chemical lavatories were groundless. It began to rain; it was that stage in the Winter when it becomes imposs- ible to remember the last day when it did not.

She never realised how short her youth had been until she was sufficiently advanced in years to admit to having had one at all. By comparison with her acquaintances she had had no adolescence whatsoever; no bad temper, no puppy love, no cider-fired groping. Having been reared in Kuala Lumpur, it struck her that the fashionable obsession among her fellow students with matters Eastern was both irrelevant and fool- hardy. She was a virgin until her twentieth year. This had never seemed odd at the time; she remembered her teenage self as having other, more important things on her mind. Then a young barrister proposed to her and took her to bed. In that order. He was still at bar school, in fact, and while uncommon- ly wealthy, far less intelligent than she. After seven months of awkward dinners *en famille* and tentative plans for their coupled future – all with a detached but nonetheless educative underlay of bed – her father was relieved to see her break off the engagement. The year after this he remarried: one Marie- Claude Beaumont. Young, pretty and Parisian, M–C was wholly welcome in Henry's view, if only because her dedica- tion to things 'feminine' provided a convenient smokescreen for her own more adventurous impulses. The two women fell into instant accord, while regarding each other's territory with affectionate dismay. Possibly because her stepmother was two years her junior, Henry bore her a sisterly love quite unlike that sense of maternal responsibility engendered by her young brother. Soon after the honeymoon her father had secured a lucrative, pre-retirement post in Paris and set up home there

19

with his young bride. After so many years in Kuala Lumpur, all his once-important English roots had withered.

Her education had been so protracted that, in her mid-thirties, this was Henry's first non-trainee post. Over the last seven years she had moved steadily away from the sight of blood and produced a doctoral thesis on the social rehabilitation of the mentally disturbed. This was a professionally sound topic, given recent health service economies. Death and a block on admissions had already reduced the occupancy of Princess Marina's to 250, but the hospital was to be axed in two years and someone had to lure, drive and settle the remaining patients into discreet corners of the community by then. Possibly thanks to her sheer innocence at the time of her interview, Henry had landed the job.

After the happy death of her engagement, Henry's only non-professional encounters with men tended towards the brief, the erratic and the uninvolved. A psychiatric don with whom she had sustained one of her more prolonged liaisons had diagnosed her apparent inability to do more than drop those men whom she bothered to pick up, as a profound amorous mistrust stemming from the abandonment by – e.g. death of – her mother during her formative years. Henry had abandoned rather than killed him on an Isle of Wight ferry the next day and returned with renewed vigour to her work. She regarded her work with unfeigned enthusiasm; the male animal so rarely matched it for intellectual or emotional stimulus that he had never presented it with a serious rival for her time. She saw no reason to allow her female acquaintances (or Hilary) a glimpse of a sexual history that she regarded as irrelevant, and was amused and only occasionally hurt by the easy decline in their curiosity. She worked a hard six-day/occasional night week, saw Hilary once a week, telephoned her father twice weekly. She went on holiday once a year, dieted every January, got by on Scotch, adventure and chocolate biscuits. She rarely smoked and she never gave lifts.


A burly six foot. Jawline. Short black hair. She never gave lifts. She pulled over and wound down the window.

'Where to?'

'Shepherds Bush? That's very kind.'

Jeans. Funny old suit jacket. Five o'clock shadow.

'Well, you'll get soaked if you wait there. Get in. Throw those things in the back.' The *raison d'être* of little yellow tart cars was that one never had room for hitch-hikers. Or was it that one only had room for one?

'How long have you been going?'

'I've only just started,' he said. 'I'd . . . er . . . I'd finished work back there and couldn't get a train home.'

'There's a tube near there, though.'

'Yes, but apparently they're still on strike.'

'Hopeless,' she said, knowing as she spoke that he was lying, that the transport strike was over. She slipped up into overdrive and they pulled past a convoy of police lorries. The rain was streaming across the glass, almost too fast for the wipers now. Work? Back there? Apart from Princess Marina's and a few piddling factories there was only the MOD place. She glanced once more at his shaved neck. Stupendous build. He looked awfully young for the SAS.

'Do you work near here too?' he asked, glancing across. He had grey eyes.

'Yeah,' she said as nonchalantly as she could. 'I'm a physiotherapist. Just spent a day at Princess Marina's.'

'Oh, right. The looney bin.'

She pulled back into the middle lane. That 'yeah' was not convincing. Drop it.

'That's the one,' she said. 'How about you?'

'Oh . . . er . . . I'm afraid I'm not allowed to say.'

SAS. Beyond question SAS.

'Sorry. How exciting.'

An understatement. This was bloody marvellous. Why had she never taken role therapy seriously?

'Cigarette?'

'No thanks, but you go ahead,' she said, pushing in the lighter button. The rain had blackened the shoulders of his jacket. Damp wool reached her nostrils and, she was prepared to swear, Old Spice. She swallowed. Her father had worn Old Spice before he met Marie-Claude. 'You're soaked,' she added. They were reaching White City, mounting the Westway.

21

'Yes, I am rather. Forgot my coat. Snow forecast for this evening.'

'I can believe that; it was freezing last night.' His cigarette smoke stung her eyes. She swung off the flyover, flew through an amber light and headed, accelerating the while, for the Holland Park roundabout. 'My brother lives near here,' she said.

'Really. Yes. I know someone up near White City.'

He shifted his position so that his knees – long legs – were now bent close to the gearstick. Oh dear. We would seem to have missed Shepherds Bush. He blew out another slow cloud of smoke and tapped out some ash. Long, thin fingers.

'Where d'you live?' he demanded.

What right have you?

'Hammersmith,' she said. 'Right on the river.'

'Show me.'

She should stop the car right now and tell him to get out. She should stab his hand with the cigarette lighter. There was an old can of anti-mugger spray somewhere. She had gin. Were there any limes?

'Two more minutes,' she said and bit her lip.

From Olympia to Holyport Road he sat, she drove without a word. The rain thickened, flattening pedestrians into doorways, mashing the accumulated dog shit on the pavements, buoying up armadas of garbage between the lines of slow-moving cars. He smoked another cigarette. She became aware of the regularity of her breathing.

She wanted to impress him with the remote control door to the car park, but there was evidently a power failure. She glanced up. Even in the downpour any lights would show. The building was blacked-out. The one unsmashed street-lamp was wired to an emergency generator. Its jaundiced glow reached the car's interior.

'We'll have to park here and make a dash for it.' She had to shout against the drumming on the roof. 'No umbrella, I'm afraid. You take that coat from the back; I'll need my hands for unlocking the door. Yup, press that button to lock up.'

She was soaked before she had even shut the driver's door. The lift was lifeless. In the darkness on the stairs she felt his hand up her skirt and heard herself laugh.

She lived in a warehouse converted into ten or so flats. Hers was on the top; a large studio made by building an extra floor beneath the tall, metal-beamed apex of the roof. She mistrusted colour and found patterns intrusive, so the walls, floor and ceilings were white. She had no need of blinds or curtains, since no one could see in. She hated clutter, so besides the bed, an overstuffed chaise-longue, a desk and a chair there was no furniture. The only frivolity was a four-foot stuffed crocodile given her – after clamorous demands – by her parents on her ninth birthday. This had a small ring through the underside of its tail by which it dangled, trophy-like, on an expanse of white wall. The high wooden doors which once swung out to a sturdy pulley and a five-storey drop to a waiting barge had been replaced by tall windowed ones and a balcony. A basket of frost-blackened ivy swung from the old pulley beam. When there was no power cut one could look from the bed out across the Thames to house lights rippling, elongated in the reservoirs at Barnes.

Something stopped. She opened her eyes and saw that it was the rain. Through a gash in the clouds she could see the moon, barely incomplete. What time? His arm lay across her breasts, his fingertips on her open armpit. She didn't move; he mustn't wake yet. The ticking of the alarm clock was distinct to her left. She tried moving her head oh so slightly and turned her eyes so far north-east that they hurt. Still she couldn't see. The corner of her mouth itched where his saliva was drying. Gingerly she slipped her left hand from under her head and brought it round to scratch. She had not taken off her watch. She twisted her wrist to catch the moonlight. Five past twelve. Happy birthday, dear Hilary, happy birthday to you! She let her arm fall to her side and the movement, the pressure on his fingertips, stirred him. He made a faint humming sound, rolled from his stomach on to his side and nestled his face into her shoulder. His breathing slowed once more. His hand now cupped her left breast and with each intake of breath she could feel the slight, resisting pressure of its weight. He breathed now through his nose, now through his mouth; the remains of a cold perhaps. His breath was hot on her collarbone. She

23

wished she were not so thin; her bones lacked padding, felt cold. She was sure that they could not be comfortable to sleep with.

His name was Andrew. He thought she was called Sandy — Sandy Marsh — and that she was sub-renting the flat of a 'really brainy' medical friend of hers who had gone to Paris for a year. She made no attempt to analyse this compulsive lie, any more than she did her stopping the car some hours ago. The earth hadn't moved. She was still Dr Henrietta Metcalfe, thirty-five, albeit with a perhaps twenty-eight-year-old stranger called Andrew who might or might not be with the SAS, with his hand on her left titty. She did enjoy, however, the faint scent of hot body and dead cigarette, and the sharp sensation that the carbines of her life had ground momentarily to this overheated standstill.

Was there a chance that he might, stroke, did she want him to stay, question mark.

She shivered. The boiler switched itself off at midnight. She touched the skin of her thigh and found gooseflesh. Glancing across at the window, she saw it was snowing . . . as he had said it would.

Carefully she slid her shoulder from under Andrew's cheek and, sitting up, reached for the duvet that had slipped away below their feet. She pulled it over the two of them and nestled back in to her pillows, staring at his sleeping face inches from her own. His head and neck were all muscle and bone; almost too firm. Even now when he was sleeping, the neck seemed tensed, braced for a blow.

He made that humming noise again and reached out a warm arm. She smiled as he groped about her thigh and ribs, trying to work out her position. She leaned over and brushed his nose with her lips.

'Hello.'

Her voice was loud against the silence and he opened his eyes too smoothly. He had been lying awake with them shut so as to fool her into admiring his sleeping form. Vain, oh vain.

'What time is it?'

'Ten past twelve.'

'Shit!'

He jumped out of bed, almost throwing the bedding off her as well.

24

'What's the matter?'

'Sorry. There was someone I was meant to meet. Can I use your 'phone?'

'The lines are still down here – they're mending them some time this week. The nearest box is at the other end of the road, by the pub.'

'Fuck.'

He pulled on his jeans, then sat on the bed to tie his laces. She would not ask if he were coming back. She *would* not.

'It's snowing,' she said. 'Take that old coat.'

'Thanks.'

Would she see it again? Don't talk to strangers. Never give lifts or you'll lose your favourite garments. He walked over to the door and coughed.

'Sorry about this. It's my . . . er . . . wife. Will you let me back in?'

'Yes. Sure.' She smiled. 'Sure.'

He was gone. But he was coming back. She threw off the duvet and groped for her dressing-gown. The candle on the table had burnt down hours ago, but there were some more in the drawer. She felt for them among the papers and safety-pins. Suddenly the fluorescent tube over the bathroom sink blinked into life. Across the river the reservoir filled with strips of guttering gold. She shut the drawer and went for a glass of water.

One arm felt sore near the top. She peered in the mirror and frowned to see a finger-shaped bruise. In the medicine cupboard there was a tube of something her father called *dentifrice des nègres*. Reaching for the cupboard door she caught her reflection: flushed, slept-in. He was coming back. Definitely. She squeezed some of the black cream on to the hurt and rubbed it in, staining the skin a brownish yellow. Then she started to wash her hands.

Did he say wife?

# Chapter Five

The window of a kerb-crawling Cortina wound down across the midnight street. A long arm came out with a bicycle horn on the end, which honked.

'Oy! Birthday boy!' the honker called out in a drama school Yiddish accent.

'Richard?'

'He pretends not to recognise his own mother!' The accent was dropped. 'Get in, Snotface, we're going for a birthday treat.'

Hilary wavered, shouting through the crossfire of a smallish blizzard. 'Oh Rich. I'd love to, but I'm expecting . . .'

'Let the joybells ring.'

'Very droll,' said Hilary, coming closer. 'I'm waiting for Rufus.'

'Whatever became of pride?'

'You win.'

As the Cortina revved, he fell into the front seat and, *Ballo in Maschera* blaring, they roared onto the Westway.


During Hilary's first college supper at Durham, he had been bullied into attending a Christian Union meeting. Richard, who had been sitting within earshot, had followed him thither, charged with a missionary spirit rather less than spiritual. They had fled to Richard's room after disgracing themselves during a three-minute silent prayer. There Hilary was introduced to the several delights of good shortbread dunked in poor sherry. He woke the next morning to find that everything suggested in Johannesburg Cream's advertising was true, and more.

Bad sherry turned to better port and still less affordable champagne. Richard's room became a rented cottage, an Austin Cambridge and a cat. Two years were mapped out by ten or so drama society productions veering from the portentous amateur to the frivolous near-professional, by two Christmases, several holiday jobs, one Grecian idyll and an emetic spell on the Edinburgh fringe. Then Hilary woke up to find that Bed, which had once loomed so large, had dwindled to amiable insignificance, leaving them the meals of the day and two second-hand suits to share. Finals revision arrived, the cat was electrocuted behind the fridge and Hilary moved back into a college room. Several years on, Richard remained a mildly jealous best friend. They shared too much knowledge for any rekindling of a love built on guile, but there was Chianti and a spontaneous bedding-down from time to reassuring time. Richard was now an actor.


They left the car in the railway executives' car park at St Pancras and walked to one of the windswept lanes to its rear. The Dazzling Leopard was housed in a tall, thin building between a disused filling station and a late Georgian house. The latter had been smartly converted by a firm of Islington solicitors who, it was rumoured, owned the neighbouring club as well.

Richard pulled out a Yale key on a synthetic furry tag and let them in. By giving each member a key and charging all drinks on a computerized credit system, the legal entrepreneurs managed to sidestep the new, stricter licensing laws. Richard remained uncertain as to how he was to pay the bill for his first year's membership. Unless another mattress commercial proved forthcoming, he would be forced to sign up for an extensive tour of East Lothian and points North.

He signed the visitors' book and they climbed the stairs from the unassuming hall to the 'party' above. They were met on the landing by the greeter, Andrea, said to be sister to one of the solicitors next door.

'Dick, darling. Kiss kiss. Oh good, and you've brought your friend.'

Andrea was also said to have been sacked from her post at a Midlands charm school for inducing the more impressionable of her charges to snort ground nutmeg. 'Coats?' she asked, waving a hand at Richard's second-hand Aquascutum and Hilary's less than spotless British Warm.

'No, thanks,' said Richard and gestured to Hilary to keep his on. 'Is Rufus here?'

'Who?'

'Never mind.'

Andrea homed in on new guests. 'Tom, darling, and little Susan. Kiss kiss. Coats?'

'Why can't I take my coat off?' asked Hilary, who was warming up fast.

'You can, but keep it with you. I didn't like to put you off, but I saw a bright red Vauxhall Cavalier discreetly parked outside with four rather insensitive looking plain-clothes men inside.' Richard signed for a brace of double gins and they pushed their way through the crowd to a newly vacant sofa.

'Cheers, darl,' said Hilary and drank.

'Cheers,' Rich returned. 'So how's the course of true love?'

'Fuck off.'

'Oh dear. We must do something there.'

'Hands off. It's my problem.'

'But I care, and he's a fully-qualified shit.'

'No, he's not. He's just, well, he's just independent.'

'You mean insufferably rude.'

'So are you when you're allowed to meet him.'

Richard snorted, then bowed to a familiar face. 'Is it just me feeling my great age,' he asked in an undertone, 'or are there an awful lot of children here tonight?'

'Children. He's barely seventeen and she could be in my 15B. In fact, I'm fairly certain she is. Oh, God!'

'Depraved, really,' continued Richard, not listening. 'Why did you ask her if Rufus was here?'

'Curiosity. I'd never thought to before, and Andrea never forgets a name. Cigarette? No, you still don't; I forgot.'

'What makes you think he comes here?' asked Hilary, trying not to look around too obviously.

'Where else is there?' asked Richard, tailing his gaze.

'Charing Cross, I suppose, Leicester Square.'

'Leicester Square?'

'Well, I do sometimes wonder whether I'm not barking up the wrong tree.'

'Women? Oh, come off it. He's far too hard-hearted; straights are all squidgy in the middle.'

'I think you're being too categorical. He might be squidgy for all I know. He is in his way.'

'Dance?'

'Oh all right.'

The Dazzling Leopard played a good selection of 'Golden Oldies', which was kind, but ultimately cruel. Nothing is more guaranteed to make night-clubbers feel their age than watching teenagers sit on the sidelines while they have a good time. After their bout of nostalgia, Hilary and Richard were driven to take refuge in the lavatories. The sweat had run into Hilary's eyes and was stinging, while Richard was on the point of collapse, having refused to shed his Aquascutum. Hilary was bent over a basin, splashing cold water onto his face, when Richard strolled out once more to find them a second round. As Hilary tried to dry himself on a hot-air machine without scorching his hair, his friend ran back in.

'Quick,' Richard said. 'Out of the window. Raid!' He hurried to the window and threw it open.

'Pull the other one, Batman,' Hilary laughed and opened the door.

The music was continuing, incongruous, while three policemen from the plain-clothes Vauxhall jostled the revellers to the far side of the room. They were only searching, no doubt, for under-age drinkers; still, Hilary retreated instinctively. As the fourth policeman turned towards him, he slammed the door and clambered out over the sill to the fire escape. Richard was waiting and yanked the window down behind him before they fled to the street. Their sprint to the car proved unnecessary but, as Richard pointed out once they were heading, Verdi-soothed, back to W12, it added to the pungent sense of living dangerously. Hilary was less certain. He had never seen a raid before. They seemed to be frequent enough, but he ventured out so rarely.

'Let's talk tomorrow,' Richard said as he pulled off the Westway onto Wood Lane. 'Do I ring you or nudge you?'

29

'Rich, you're sweet.' Hilary laid a hand on his arm. This always happened after nights out *à deux*. 'But I've got twenty assessments to write before school.'

'Oh, go on. Live dangerously.'

'It wouldn't be fun.'

'Thanks.'

'You know what I mean. I'd be all cross and you'd want . . .'

'Yes. I know.'

'But thanks for the outing. Raid'n'all.'

'Shucks, Homer, it was nothin'. I'll drop you off.'

'No, it's OK. The snow's stopped. I'll walk from here, then you needn't do a turn. It's not far.' Richard made no protest, so Hilary opened his door and stepped out into the snow.

'See you Wednesday,' Richard called out.

'Why Wednesday?'

'Our class.'

'Oh. Yes. Night.'

He waved as Richard sped away, then thrust his hands deep in his pockets and shuddered. It was about two o'clock and he had to be bright-eyed and bushy-tailed for Junior Drama Group in six or so hours. He trudged homeward . . .

That sound again. Hilary stopped. A chance peace lay over the road, save for an unmistakable crying from the subway. Curious, he walked back and took a few paces into the entrance. There in a corner lay a carrycot, audibly inhabited. The occupant had been crying for some time and the repeated, jerky wail was growing hoarse. He started towards it, then froze. It was obviously a trap. Someone had set it down there, in full view of the pavement, and was waiting out of sight with monkey wrench in hand. Mr Jarvis, the school caretaker, had been beaten up and robbed down there only a few days ago. Hilary turned back along the pavement. As if anyone would leave a baby lying there on such a night! The idea was risible. He was plainly drunk; normally he would never have been so gullible.

No sooner had he crossed under the flyover, however, than a gin-fed conscience began to nag him. The idea was not *so* risible. One did read of unwanted children being abandoned. Last month there had been a case of a mother whose daughter was being so badly beaten by her lover that she left her on a

Circle Line train in the hope that she would thus find a more loving home.

Heart in mouth, Hilary crossed Wood Lane and made for the other end of the subway. This way, if there was anyone lying in wait with a monkey wrench, he might make good his retreat before they saw him. He slowed his pace as he entered the tunnel, and moved on tip-toe. Gingerly he peered round the corner, his cheek on the icy grime of the tiles. No one. The carrycot held single sway. Embarrassed at his cowardice, he ran to rescue it. He bent forward and peered in.

A small, sparsely haired head lay on the pillow and two wretchedly small hands worked spasmodically at the flannel sheeting beneath them. The skin was slightly dusky. Hilary reached out and touched the baby's scalp. Startled perhaps, the crying ceased. There were two little pants, then it resumed with renewed strength. A youngest child and cousinless, Hilary had never so much as felt new-born skin. He had seen the things being wheeled about, of course, and had seen them having their nappies changed or their mouths charged with sodden rusks in advertisements, but this kind of immediate contact was wholly new and, were he less intoxicated, distinctly frightening. He lifted the carrycot and gave it an experimental swing, but the hoarse yells redoubled, so he set it down again. He felt around the blankets; there was a small white teddy, but not the note that he had expected. Such discoveries were meant to arrive with a monogrammed shawl, or at least a box of distinguishing trinkets. A note reading, 'My name is Felix. Love me,' would at least have marshalled a sense of purpose. He continued to grope and found a full bottle, which tentatively he set down by the baby's lips. There were footsteps behind him. He glanced up to see an old woman shuffling past with two full carrier bags. Perhaps she would claim it, or at least give vent to some kind of helpful indignation. Hilary prepared to be embarrassed. Instead she stopped, peered over his shoulder into the carrycot and said,

'Ah! Inny sweet! Inny lovely! What's he called, then?'

In Kuala Lumpur he had been given an orphan guinea-pig to rear with milk from a dropper, a fluffed-up mahogany animal he had called Dan.

'Erm . . . oh yes. He's called Dan. Daniel, actually, but we just call him Dan.'

'Ah. Dan.' She tried the name out. '*Dan*. Sweet.' So saying, she shuffled on down the tunnel.

Hilary watched her, listening to the slap of her rotten slippers on the wet tiles, then realized that the baby had fallen quiet. He looked down and saw that the obliging creature was sucking greedily on the teat of the bottle.

'Sweet,' he tried, then, 'Absurd,' he said to himself. With the sigh of the whist player who finds he has been dealt an assortment of twos and threes, he lifted the carrycot and headed for the North Pole.

He let himself in and climbed the stairs to his flat, exhausted. Vacantly, he set down the carrycot on his desk beside the empty whisky bottle and began to open out the sofa into a bed. His eye caught the telephone answering machine – a paternal present that predated the watches – and saw that a single call was recorded. He sat on the bed and pressed the play button. The tape rewound, there was the usual bleep, then:

'Hi, Hil! It's Rufus. Look, I'm really sorry I didn't make it over to you this evening . . . erm . . . something came up. But look, happy birthday and . . . erm . . . you don't look a day over twenty-two. No, I mean it. Honestly . . . erm . . . Look, I'll ring you, OK? 'Bye.'

Resenting the inane grin that crept to his lips, Hilary pulled on his pyjamas, brushed his teeth and turned out the light. He was hovering at the borders of sleep, starting to feel the mattress heave drunkenly beneath him, when the darkness was pierced by a baby's cry. Too tired to think, too drunk to react on any but a primitive level, he rose and walked over to the desk. He reached beneath the diminutive bedding and pulled out the complaining inmate.

'Here, Dan. Here. Shut up,' he murmured. 'Ssh.' He clambered under the duvet once more with the baby beside him. The cries were replaced almost at once by breathing worthy of a dirty phone caller.

Tomorrow was another day. He would think about things tomorrow.

# Chapter Six

As Rufus found his way to the darkened hall, the lights came on. Behind him the lift apologized to the ignored commands of the past hours, opening and closing its doors before it glided with an under-oiled sigh towards the upper storeys. Snow was drawn into his face as he swung open the front door. In the chilled flurry the street—lamp seemed less feeble. At the far end of the street the bulb in the telephone kiosk was flickering out a lonely code. Wincing against the cold, he strode towards it. The machine was of an unfamiliar design, presumably one of the few anti-vandal models set up before the communications strike last year.

He pushed in a coin and dialled, numb fingers fumbling. The answering tone sounded five times.

'Hi. Look, I'm . . .' Rufus began, then cursed and fell silent. He stared at a crisp bag waltzing on the draughty floor, then waited twenty seconds. A thin, high buzz sounded in his ear and he spoke again, awkwardly. 'Hi Hil! It's Rufus. Look, I'm really sorry I didn't make it over to you this evening . . . erm . . . something came up. But look, happy birthday and . . . erm . . . you don't look a day over twenty-two. No, I mean it. Honestly . . . erm . . . Look, I'll ring you, OK? 'Bye.' He replaced the receiver. After a succession of clicks, he scooped six coins from the returned coin slot. 'Nice to have friends,' he said.

Faint lights and lowered voices came from The Bird in Hand. He pushed at the door, but it was locked. The voices dropped altogether. After a pause, a woman's voice – he could see her on the other side of the frosted glass – asked, 'That you, officer?'

'No,' he offered. 'It's me. It's Rufus.'

'It's all right,' she laughed, 'only Roof.' She unbolted the door and pulled it open a foot. 'Come on in. Fucking brass monkeys out there tonight.'

There were perhaps twenty-five drinkers arranged across the murky space. He ignored them, walking straight to the bar, and they began to talk again. He ordered a Scotch, paid and sat on a stool near a radiator. The spirit burned pleasantly in his chest. He had eaten nothing since a mobile breakfast. He had banked on the Phillips woman paying for her lesson in cash, but she had said she only had cheques and wouldn't that do. He had told her to wait and pay him double in cash next week. So no lunch.

He ran a hand through his hair. The melting snow sent a bitter trickle down his bare neck and he shuddered.

Sandy, the physiotherapist girl . . . woman . . . had startled him. He wasn't quite sure why she had given him a lift; he didn't have his thumb out. He had left Mrs Phillips in bed, bathed, dressed and set out for the tube as usual when there, out of the thickening rain, came an attractive woman in a rusty Spitfire who offered him a lift. Stupid of him not to tell her what he did. She probably had some tacky military fantasy woven round him now. It was just that, 'I'm a piano teacher' seemed so pathetic and, 'I occasionally screw my pupils' even more so. Also he was paranoid about giving details of his work. He had been signing on while working for cash for over a year now. It was said that those who were caught out were always taken in the first few weeks, making beginners' mistakes, but still he couldn't relax. In his heart he felt sure that the DHSS would be lenient with him; even with the dole, his income was erratic. After arguments with Hilary, he had spent days on a ration of cold baked beans and cream crackers.

How could this Sandy *trust* him so? Possessiveness was common enough, but trust was not something to which he was accustomed. She had even let him walk off with her coat. He stroked the sleeve. A good coat. She trusted him to return. He watched a woman set coins thumping from a fruit machine and was tempted to walk away, just to prove Sandy wrong.

34

Then again, the loss of a good coat was something she could well afford. The flat. The car. She probably paid enough national insurance for two.

Wonderfully strong arms. Squash-player arms. A mid-twenties body betrayed solely by her neck; he had counted the rings – one per decade. She lacked Hilary's air of calculated walk-on-me devotion, so her trust must stem from stupidity. She was only a physiotherapist, which was little better than a glorified masseuse. Stupidity or innocence. There were too many surprise lines in her face for either. From the moment she had pressed in the cigarette lighter for him, he had noticed an air of quiet control. Could she be lying too? The thought was intensely arousing. He shifted forward on his stool and swigged the last of his Scotch.

There was an itching above his wrist. He rubbed it hard, then pushed back his sleeve and found a deep scratch about two inches long. At the deepest end blood was seeping up. The itching was the formation of a scab, which he had just rubbed away. He licked at the blood, then asked to be let out.


'Hello?' said the poised, low voice in the grille. A spotlight in the wall clicked on in his face and Rufus stared into it.

'Hi,' he said. 'It's Andrew.'

'You took your time.'

'The 'phone was bust. I had to walk up to the Broadway.'

'Get in the lift and press button four.'

# Chapter Seven

Sumitra Sharma first knew the meaning of blind devotion when hiding in a school lavatory on her eleventh birthday. Tamsin Clark, who was pretty by white standards save for the web of metal clips and staples that held her teeth together, had commented loudly on the fact that she was remarkably short for an eleven-year-old. Her sidekick Kerry, who was monstrous plain by comparison, but whose wit was generally sharper, had expanded on this to suggest that Asian mothers pissed on their children's breakfast cereal in order to stunt their growth and yellow their skins. Sumitra had retorted that men preferred their women delicate and that her race scorned such abominations as breakfast cereal. A savage chase had ensued, which was how she had come to see him receiving a black eye from a cricket ball. She didn't see the blow, which made the emotional revelation all the sweeter.

She had darted through the various skirmishes and ball-games, leaving Tamsin and Kerry swearing and jeering as they were variously struck and kicked in their flagging pursuit. With a glance behind her, she fled into the boys' lavatories. She ran panting down the line of wash-basins, past the baby urinals, through a scrum of magazine-ogling youths who sent up a cheer, and into the safety of a full-size cubicle whose door she slammed and bolted. She stood on the seat to keep her feet out of arms's reach, and waited, listening. No footsteps came after her and she heard the boys shambling noisily away. Carefully she changed the position of her sandals on her filthy perch and forced the arrow slit of a window open.

She had meant to scan the crowd for her pursuers but found

herself looking him full in the face. He was finishing a conversation with someone at the common room window above her.

'Yes. That's fine, Pat,' he had said with a dazzling smile. 'OK. Bye.'

Then he had turned away and been smitten by the hurtling ball. The ball was coming from exactly opposite her window, so that one moment she was staring at his bright, hopeful face and the next she saw him fall like a dropped rag soldier.

This was how Sumitra Sharma came to love him. In her way.

# Chapter Eight

Hilary opened his eyes. One leg and one arm dangled over the edge of the bed into a bitterly cold draught. It was one minute to eight. As on even the most reluctant mornings, he had woken seconds before the alarm, which entailed a tense little wait for the official summons to rise. There was a damp patch under his cheek where he had been dribbling. The light under the curtain had the crude brilliance peculiar to snow scenes. He pulled his straying limbs back under the duvet and shut his eyes once more. After perhaps thirty seconds the German alarm clock let out a finely honed whine, which he stopped with a well-practised tap of a finger. Moments later a Japanese timer socket – courtesy Dad, Christmas 1985 – activated a cassette-player. Then, as the nuns wondered how to solve a problem like Maria, they were joined by an indignant bellow somewhere behind Hilary's head. A baby.

Oh Lord! The baby.

The baby had wet himself, and the bed, and – it became alarmingly clear as Hilary rushed him with an oath or two to the bathroom – had not been so ungenerous as to stop there. The next ten minutes were rather like dealing with a blind-drunk lover or a loose-bowelled red setter; it was surprising what one could accomplish with gritted teeth, warm soapy water and a little initiative. It was only once Dan (who had indeed proved to be male) was back in his carrycot gurgling, sweetly (and expensively) powdered and freshly swaddled in an off-cut of an old towel, and once the sullied sheets had been flung into the twin-tub, that Hilary had time to wonder where he had learned to change a nappy so well.

He did something about washing himself, then cleaned the feeding bottle with boiling water, which he presumed to take some kind of sterilising effect, filled it with milk and returned to the bedroom with that and a glass of orange juice. The bottle arrived with seconds to spare as the gurgles were tingeing a pale shade of rage. Hilary held the baby in what seemed a comfortable position for both and put the bottle to the puckering lips.

'There you are, Dan,' he tried. Then, more daring, 'that's it . . . er . . . darling.'

As one set of astonishingly small fingers rose to rest on his own around the bottle, he reflected that the feasting animal in his lap was not unappealing and, were it not for the horrendous responsibility, not much more bother than a fairly demanding guinea-pig. Dan pulled back from the teat, panting slightly, and stared hard at the face of his feeder. For all the appalling newness of the skin, his general mien was one of extreme old age. The puffy eyes were so brown as to verge on black. The few rings of hair were also dark. The features were Anglo-Saxon enough, but the skin was not. Caucasian babies seemed so pink and blotchy, their faces a pattern of unapproachable delicacy; this face looked as warm as it felt, somewhere between brown eggshell and digestive biscuit. The bottle was guided back to the mouth and the impromptu breakfast continued to a bubbling close.

'There, Dan,' said Hilary, wiping away a milky moustache with the edge of a towel, 'All gone? Good boy. Who's a good boy? There!'

He stood with his precious bundle and walked, still naked, to pull open a kitchen curtain with his spare hand. The roof of the Sharmas' garage down below was thick with snow and several inches of the stuff lay on the surrounding houses. Hedges were walls and parked cars Arctic tumuli. The traffic on North Pole Road would be swimming through a liquefying brown slurry by now. The grit-spreaders were bound to be on strike.

'Look, Dan. Snow,' he enthused, turning so that Dan could face the scene and feeling the baby's warmth on his rapidly chilling chest. Dan seemed about to smile, but his lips wavered the wrong side of mirth and he appeared to be holding his breath. With the same mysterious (television acquired?) knowledge that had guided his hands in the bathroom, Hilary held him against a shoulder and gently patted his back. Head awobble, Dan let out a fruity belch, absurdly baritone in one of his size. 'Who's a good boy,' praised Hilary, feeling terribly gifted of a sudden. '*Clever* darling! Any more down there? Eh?'

He rubbed the little spine again and was rewarded with a flurry of hot vomit down his back and what sounded distinctly like a laugh. In the living room the Mother Superior bellowed 'Climb Ev'ry Mountain' in a supportive fashion.


He had taken the clinic's address from the telephone directory and battled through the snow on foot. Apart from one accompanying a pregnant woman, he was the only man in the waiting room.

'Have you an appointment?'

'Well no, but I . . .'

'Take a ticket from the dispenser and come forward when your number comes up,' said the receptionist. 'Thank you. Have you made an appointment, Madam?'

Hilary tore a ticket from the dispenser; it was number 74. He glanced around him and eventually made out a dial in the shadows over the reception desk. It read 62. He heaved Dan's carrycot over to the payphone and pulled out a coin. Then he saw that no wire joined the handset to the machine. He returned to the queue for the receptionist. She seemed not to recognize him.

'Yes? Have you got an appointment?'

'No, but I . . .'

'Take a ticket from . . .'

'I have, but my number won't come up for ages and I'm going to be late for work. I'm a teacher, you see.'

Several women looked up from their dog-eared magazines.

'Couldn't you 'phone the school?'

'It's been vandalized.'

'Are you sure?'

'Yes. And there weren't any kiosks outside.'

'Then you'll have to come back tomorrow. I can fit you in at five.'

40

'I have to work then too,' he lied. 'It's really very urgent.'

'Perhaps your wife, then . . .'

'I'm not married.'

More dog-eared looks. Luckily Daniel was asleep. If he lets the side down by crying, thought Hilary, I'll join in.

'I'll just deal with this lady. Could you step aside a moment?' Hilary stepped aside as she turned her dully inquiring gaze on the woman behind him. The woman had made an appointment and walked with an air of lofty wisdom straight through. The receptionist turned back to him. She lowered her voice and confided, without a smile,

'If you go through door number seven and wait, Matron will see you next.'

'Thanks,' he said, with a relieved smile. 'Thanks a lot.' He started forward but she checked him.

'What?'

'Leave a fiver in the drawer.'

The room was windowless. There were a desk, an examination bed and two chairs. Leaving the carrycot on the bed, he sat on a chair, pulled out his wallet and opened the drawer. A five pound note and a few pound coins – he assumed from the previous queue-jumpers – lay there already. Suddenly indignant, he shut the drawer and replaced his money.

He waited in the fluorescent light and rehearsed the meeting to come. He would explain how and where he had found the baby. She would want to know what Dan had had to eat and whether he seemed to have suffered from his exposure. He would probably have to sign something and then he could walk out a free man and catch the bus to school. There was always the possibility that he would have to go to the police to make a statement. Abandoning a child was almost certainly a crime, after all. He hoped that a signature for Matron would suffice their needs. Figures of authority invariably had him tongue-tied with unspecific guilt.

Matron was nothing if not authoritative. She breezed in and filled the chair he had vacated. He sat across the desk from her:

'Good morning, Mr . . .?'

'Metcalfe.'

'Mr Metcalfe. And what seems to be the matter? Is it your wife?'

41

'No. Er . . .'

She followed Hilary's gaze to the bed and the carrycot.

'Ah. Fine,' she said and pulled out a form from a folder. 'We haven't seen you before, have we?'

'No.'

'Just a few details then.' She spoke slowly as she wrote in block capitals, 'M.E.T.C.A.L.F.E. First name?'

'Hilary.'

'No. *Your* name.'

'As I said, Hilary.'

'Unusual in a man,' she continued, unperturbed. 'H.I.L-.A.R.Y. Age?'

'Twenty-five.'

'Two. Five. NHS number?' He told her. 'And address?' He told her this also. 'Fine.' She wrote, then looked up. 'Now the child. Sex?'

'He's a boy.'

'Male. Age?'

'I couldn't say exactly.'

'Well roughly, then.'

Her tone was impatient. He guessed in a wild effort to please her. Unspecifically guilty.

'Five weeks?'

'Name?'

'Well . . .' He tried to laugh. She would relax and then he could explain everything. 'Well, I've been calling him Dan after a guinea-pig I once had.' She didn't laugh.

'Christened Dan or Daniel?'

'Oh, I don't think he's been christened.'

'You don't seem very sure about your child, Mr Metcalfe.'

'Actually, he's not mine; I found him last night. I say I don't think he's been christened because I get the feeling that his parents, well one of his parents was a Hindu or a Muslim.' She looked up as if to say, 'And I'm the Spirit of Bali Ha'i.' Faltering, he went on. 'I simply brought him . . . I mean . . . I thought.'

'You thought you could just dump him on us and we'd shove him in a state home pending adoption and that would be that, eh?'

'No. Look, you really don't seem . . .'

42

Matron clicked the cap back onto her pen. 'Well, I hate to disappoint you, Mr Metcalfe, but that's not the way we work. Leave him on your doorstep, did she?'

'I found him in a subway off Wood Lane, as a matter of fact,' he said, the previous night sounding increasingly unlikely.

'Mr Metcalfe. Hilary.' She gave a horrible simper which he took for a professional reassurance tactic. 'You can trust me. We needn't know her name. She obviously can't look after Dan and hoped that you could. Are you unemployed?'

'No. I teach at the Scrubbs Secondary.'

'Pity. If you were on supplementary benefit we could have found you a daily minder. Meanwhile you must read this and this to make sure you feed and dress the poor mite properly – no skimmed milk and so forth – and if you fill out this AP57 we can set the ball rolling for an adoption. It won't be quick, mind.'

'But this is absurd. Don't you understand? It, I mean, *he* isn't my baby.'

'Then why did you give *it* a name?'

'I couldn't call him nothing.'

'Some manage. We've had little girls who think their name is "Oi" or "You". Do you honestly expect me to believe that you found a child ready equipped with carrycot, nappies, bottle and baby-gro, gave it a name and didn't bother to report your discovery to the police?'

'I didn't find him until last night.'

'Mr Metcalfe,' she sighed, 'we have a lot of patients waiting. I'll take Dan through for weighing and a check-up, then you must bring him back in a fortnight. Vaccination details are in that red pamphlet I've given you.' She rose and carried Dan to the door. He started to cry and she stopped and reached a hand into his bedding. 'When did you last change him?'

'Breakfast. Eight o'clock.'

'I'll get them done again for you now. These nappies are far too large, by the way. They'll chafe his thighs. If you're such a busy man, buy some disposables. Just a matter of interest,' she added. 'What have you been feeding him?'

'Cow's milk,' said Hilary.

'And he was sick?'

'Yes. Very.'

43

'Of course he was. It must have been a shock after mother's own. We'll give you enough formula for a day or two, but then you'll have to get in your own supplies.'

She opened the door and Hilary rose with thoughts of flight. 'Don't run away,' she called over her shoulder so that all the waiting room could hear. 'Abandoning a child is an offence against decency, Mr Metcalfe.'

As the door swung behind her, Dan mouthed a sound through his tears, one tiny fist grappling the air above his pillow. It sounded suspiciously like 'Dada'. Hilary sank back on his chair. The walls of Fate seemed to be closing in.


Two and a half hours later he was back at his desk. Beside him Dan was breathing heavily from the carrycot as he slept off his lunchtime feed. Hilary had stopped at a working telephone on the way home to call school and excuse himself from morning classes. Henry would write him an official-looking note if he asked her sweetly enough.

For the present, Dan would seem to be his responsibility. He had ceased fuming at the matron's aggressive misunderstanding; he was a coward and there an end. The burden was not so onerous. He could buy him food, disposable nappies and a few clothes, marking them down to rare charity. There was a crèche where he could leave the dear boy beside the sick-room at school. Colleagues might look askance, but that had never bothered him greatly. Henry had left a message on his answering machine saying she would drop by that evening. If there were any problem about leaving so new a child at the crèche, he could get her to sign some doctorly form to help find him a day nurse.

The door-bell rang. His landlady, Mrs Sharma, stood there, her nylon wraps vivid against the grey of melting snow. Her hands were pressed together in greeting. Hilary had read a teach-oneself course on *Understanding Your Hindu Neighbours*; he pressed his hands together also.

'*Namaskaras Shrimati Sharma*,' he said, smiling.

'Hello, Hilary,' she replied. Beneath her *sari* he could see the toes of her Wellington boots. 'Forgive me for intruding like this.'

'Not at all. Come in.'

She hesitated, seeming embarrassed. 'Well, you see . . .' Her eyes kept flicking to her left.

'No, honestly. I'm not busy. Come in out of the cold.' He stood back to welcome her, but she stayed put.

'I saw the baby,' she said at last and Hilary felt himself flush.

'Well, yes. Isn't it extraordinary?' was all he could find to say.

'I thought perhaps . . .' She reached out to her left and wheeled a cot into the doorway. It was almost new and filled with baby clothes and nursery equipment. She seemed painfully shy about presenting him with the things. 'These are all Sumitra's old clothes and so on. We have no use for them now, of course, and I thought . . .'

'That's terribly kind of you. He's not really mine, you know, I . . .'

'Yes, I guessed. You are very good to take him in.'

'Well, I daresay he won't be with me for long. I should find him a proper home.'

'I'm sure your home is very proper.'

'Well. I dunno.' Hilary laughed. Mrs Sharma was a grave woman. Her knowledge of English was as near perfect as that of her garrulous husband, who had explained this with a proud reference to her superior education, yet she was habitually restrained. However, on the first day of the term, when her daughter Sumitra had joined one of his classes, she had smiled very slightly, said how glad she was that he would be teaching her child and asked him to call her Shanti. He did his best, but first-name terms were awkward to sustain with one so reserved. It was clear from their refusal to let Sumitra go to swimming or drama classes, and their insistence that she swelter through gym lessons in a thick, chaste tracksuit, that their Hinduism was staunchly orthodox.

'Would you like to come upstairs and see him?' he asked.

'Oh. Could I?' She smiled for the second time in their acquaintance. 'Only if it is no bother,' she went on, and followed him up the musty stairs to the flat.

Dan stirred as they approached the cot, and yawned. Hilary reached in and lifted him out. The baby was only just old enough to keep his neck straight, and his huge head wobbled as he stared, drooling, at Mrs Sharma. Instead of cooing, or immediately holding out her hands to take him, she let out a sharp cry and bit the back of her hand to suppress the sound. Her eyes were round with surprise. Slowly she lowered her hand, her lower lip trembling. She murmured something in Gujurati and seemed about to smile again.

'He is perfect,' she said, turning her face up to Hilary's but keeping her eyes on the child.

'Would you like to hold him?'

He held Dan out to her. She said nothing but reached out and took him closely in her arms. Dan lay breathing like a sleeper with a head cold and stared at her hard.

'He's studying my *tilah*,' she said. 'He wants to know about my third eye.' She reached up a hand and touched the red circle on her brow with a long-nailed forefinger, then, slowly slowly she brought the finger down to touch his forehead. Then she laughed, truly laughed and held him against her shoulder. Rocking slowly from one foot to the other she whispered, '*Charulata. Namaskaras charulata.*' Within seconds Dan was asleep again.

'He knows the real thing when he finds it,' said Hilary, feeling a pang of jealousy at her sureness of touch. She either ignored this or didn't hear, and laid the baby back in the carrycot.

'How will you find time to look after him?' she asked softly.

'There's a crêche at school. It's only for a few days – just until they can arrange an adoption.'

'But he's a *charulata* – you would say a godsend. Every day is important with an honoured guest.'

'Well, that's as maybe, but I have to work. He seems to sleep most of the time anyway and I could pop in to see him between classes.'

'There would be so many fearful noises. There would be other, older children. He would not sleep.' Hilary made a noise of helplessness and Mrs Sharma went on, lowering her deep eyes in humility. '*Shri Metcalfe*. Hilary. Would you let me look after him? I have so little to do. Bharat deals with all the customers and his cousin helps him. All I have to do is wash the floor at night and cook. If you did not mind me sitting here, I could come up with my sewing while you were out at school and watch over him.'

'But that would be a dreadful imposition.'

'Sorry?'

'I mean you couldn't possibly. Your own children . . . er . . .
cooking. I really couldn't let . . .'

'I have nothing to do.' Her brown gaze, intensified by the
carmine dot, was full upon him. 'After *puja*, I feed my family,
then Bharat opens shop and Sumitra runs off to school.
Cooking for the day never takes more than one hour. Otherwise I wash the floor at six and we go to the Gujurati Centre
for prayers at seven. I listen to the radio. I sew. I have asked
Bharat many times, but he will not let me work in the shop.'

'But your other daughter – sorry, I can't remember – yes,
Kamala. What about her?'

There was a brief flare of anger in her voice as she said,
'Kamala has left us. She is not our child now.'

Feeling awkward, Hilary looked back at Dan. Once more
suppliant, she continued, 'Please Hilary. It would give me so
much pleasure.'

'Well certainly. If you really want to.' It was hopeless to
resist. 'It's just that it seems . . .'

'Oh thank you,' she exclaimed and, in a moment of uncharacteristic abandon, she seized and wrung his hand. 'Thank
you, Hilary!'

'Not at all.' He started towards the stairs to show her out.
She followed him down to the hall then stopped with her hand
on the door.

'Do you have to go out this afternoon?'

'Actually yes. I got off school this morning, but I have to be
there by two and I won't be back until four.'

'That's perfect. I shall fetch my sewing then come back. You
are sure you do not mind?'

'Not in the least. On the contrary, it's sweet of you to be
such a help,' he assured her. 'I'll make up a bottle before I go,'
he continued, determined that she should not have all the fun
to herself.

# Chapter Nine

The drift did not seem too deep, so she edged the Spitfire into its midst. Something protested loudly in the bodywork; she threw the gears into reverse and touched on the accelerator, but that only made the sound worse. Henry cut the engine, leaving the radio playing. She glanced behind her – this was how they set ambushes – but the slip road was deserted. She reached under the seat for her spade and climbed out. A catering-size can that had once held 'Jam/Red/ZP794' had wedged itself between the front bumper and the pile of boxes, chicken bones and discarded vegetable matter. She swung the spade at the offending can a few times and dislodged it. Then she shovelled and kicked the half-frozen heap of refuse to one side. If she mounted the verge she would get through.

Once clear, she accelerated, remembering that she was in a good mood. Irritated by the short story, she rejected the radio in favour of a reconditioned Glenn Gould recording of Bach. *The Art of the Fugue*.

It was worryingly simple to play Sandy Marsh. After the initial lies, the new persona had seemed to well from her inside. With the simple words came simple thoughts and from there on it was ... well, simple. Insulting, really. Despite her satisfaction, Henry needed to remind herself that there were higher pleasures. Half the sweetness of mischief lay in its undertow of guilt.

Bach's cool equations and the newly-washed lab coat folded on the passenger seat lent her a bogus detachment with which to survey her intoxicated joy. In little more than twelve hours she had stopped the car to pick up a young man whom she had never met professionally, let alone in a drawing room. She had encouraged him to abuse her body. She had degraded her status for his pleasure and had lied about her intellect for her own. Now that it seemed likely that his occupation had little to do with serving the common good or ennobling the well-informed spirit, and that she was helping him deceive his wife, she felt big. She felt big, street-wise, sassy and . . . she yawned . . . and worn to a smug ravelling.

'I want to come back tonight', said Andrew.

'Good,' said Sandy.

'You'll be in, then?'

'Yes. What time can I expect you?'

'I can't say. But I'll come.'

'Eightish or much later?'

'I said I'll come. I'll ring you.'

'I'd better have your number too, in case I'm late.'

'No.'

'But then . . .'

'Sorry. You can't call me. I'll come. OK?'

Sandy had sung in the bath. Henrietta Metcalfe *never* sang in the bath. Henrietta Metcalfe began to seem faintly drab.


Princess Marina's was built on a hill. Prime real estate, given that it was the only half-habitable spot in the area. Already bulldozers were digging foundations where the playing fields had been. Fern Farm: a luxury development for first-time buyers. Young professional couples would be flocking here in search of homes. In one corner of the site, in the shade of an old cedar, thirty-five fibreglass Georgian porticos were stacked, their white, cleanly moulded forms visible beneath a sheet of mud-flecked plastic. It was said that, if squared off, and if the Italianate towers were laid on their sides, the hospital would cover four times the area of Buckingham Palace. A senior registrar at a sherry party had once told her the number of miles of corridor. Henry had forgotten the exact figure, but it was longer than the statistic for the V. and A. or Harrods. Aerial photographs showed a vast square around a central courtyard; a red brick fortress with a bulky outcrop of hall, gateway, and towers in each corner.

Over the past five years the number of working wards had decreased steadily. Within the echoing, often precarious shell of the building, the territory of hospital functions had retreated to one side of the square, itself the stature of a sizable grammar school. Two of the other sides stood empty, windows smashed, paint peeling in broad scabs, awaiting demolition. The third housed a police dog training centre. The beasts were kennelled in the upper storey and by day the halls below resounded to savage barking and the patter and thud of paws as they climbed ladders and leaped over walls. Henry had filed a complaint that the baying upset many patients and kept them awake at night, but her letter had ricocheted around police and medical departments until a ministerial thrust in Whitehall had sent it back to her desk, resealed, unanswered and laced over by rubber stamps.

'Dr Metcalfe, thank goodness! We didn't think that you could come up till this afternoon.'

'Well, Bateman said it was urgent. Is it?'

'Rather. Yes. It's Percy – Mr Fleischmann.' Staff Nurse Sadler's face was pretty and tense. Henry was amused by encounters with Staff Nurse Sadler, as she spoke like one half of a dialogue in a doctors-and-nurses romance. 'There was some trouble last night. He seems to have nagged some of the others into attacking him. We found him in an awful state in one of the bathrooms this morning.'

'You don't know who it was?'

'No. He won't say and they're all playing innocent. He was getting on so well that Dr Jonas had him taken off trifluoperazeine.'

'When?'

'Yesterday was his first day without it.'

'Dr Jonas was wrong. Put Percy right back on it.'

'Oh. But . . .'

'Mr Fleischmann is registered as my patient, not Dr Jonas's. Put Percy back on, but lower the dosage by two hundred. It was too high, which was why we weren't getting through. I'll go and see him. Is he on his own?'

'Yes. Room D. The second on the left at the end.'

Henry walked the length of the ward. The cold sun through the high windows had striped the floor and walls. The peace was astonishing. At a table by the last bed on the left, Mrs Lewin was completing a jigsaw of Mrs Siddons' Lady Macbeth by Fuseli, her free hand tapping busily on an ample knee. She looked up briefly, to stare at Henry without recognition.

'Who is it?'

'Hello, Mr Fleischmann. It's Dr Metcalfe. Can I come in?'

'Wipe your feet.'

'Will do.' She let herself into the small yellow room. Percy Fleischmann was sitting on his bed in dressing-gown and slippers. There was a bandage around his head and he had a black eye. 'You look the worse for wear,' she said, pulling up a stool and sitting down.

'Lick my bum,' said Percy Fleischmann. Henry consulted his file.

'It says here you used to work in the post office at Bethnal Green, Percy. Were you happy there?'

'All lies,' sang Percy. 'The stupid slut put that down when I'd expressly told her that I held a very prominent position in Whitehall which I am not at liberty to disclose.'

'Really? Whitehall?'

'That is correct.'

'Splendid. Then perhaps you could tell me why the hospital is being closed down when there's nowhere else for you all to go?'

'Don't be absurd, girl. I said first class and stop writing when I'm talking to you.'

'Whoever hurt you last night was obviously very cross about something. Did you start threatening them with your blacklist again? Because you talked all about that with Dr Jonas and you had promised him you took no more interest in reprisals and had handed the entire affair over to someone less important.'

'Dr Jonas knows nothing of my affairs.' Mr Fleischmann who, though strongly built gave an abiding impression of impotence, looked over glasses that were not there. 'It's becoming rapidly clear that you know even less than Dr Jonas.' He had arrived three months ago after attacking a fellow clerk and breaking her nose while trying to post her through the sorting office window. Four days before this his wife had left him for another man and taken their only child.

'Who hurt you, Percy?'

'She was the daughter of Abashag the Shumanite.'

'Please tell me, because I'd like to have a word with them.'

'Lick my bum lick my bum lick my bum lick my bum,' said Percy.

As Henry was handing back the file to Staff Nurse Sadler, Percy ran out of his room, yelled 'bum' at the top of his voice and upended the tray on which Mrs Lewin had so nearly completed her jigsaw. He cried and Mrs Lewin started to laugh. Staff Nurse Sadler clicked her tongue and, having excused herself prettily to Dr Metcalfe, ran to prevent an ugly scene.

# Chapter Ten

Hilary slung his briefcase over his handlebars, turned on his Walkman and set out. It was a selection from *Carousel*. The side began, ironically enough, with *When the Children Are Asleep*. Henry was always telling him how dangerous it was to ride with a headful of music. He couldn't see that it was any worse than her driving with a carful and besides, even at a high volume setting he could still hear conversation on the pavements and the tooting of horns.

He wondered how Mrs Sharma had seen him with Dan. She must have been spying. The interest she showed was unnaturally keen in a mother of two. Surely the child wasn't her own? Quite apart from the fact that she had shown no signs of being in a suitable condition over the past year, the Sharmas had only daughters; Hindus favoured any son that came their way, as cruelly as any other Eastern sect.

Half-closing his eyes in preparation for the customary handfuls of gravel, he gritted his teeth and charged across the area of broken bottles and brawling youth that rejoiced in the name of playground. Keats comprehension with the delinquents would be followed by Lady Macbeth with the partially disturbed.

He locked his bike up in the music block. When one of the pianos had been vandalized beyond recognition last year, the practice room which had been its home became a staff box room; a lockable haven of semi-security for large valuables. It was after chaining his bike to the radiator in there that Hil had first glimpsed Rufus.

As he came into the corridor he had seen him open wide a

door to release little Sumitra Sharma from her piano lesson. Their eyes met for a brief almost smiling hello, then Rufus let in another pupil and shut the door once more. Later that morning, before Junior Drama Club, Hilary had returned to the music block on a quest for chime bars. He had been about to send one of his several pets to fetch them when he recalled that they were locked in the practice room containing the unfamiliar piano teacher. Only half-admitting this to himself, he had left the children doing warm-up exercises with Pat Casals.

He paused outside the door, waiting for a break in the childishly laboured arpeggios. When none proved forthcoming, he knocked. The music stopped and a stool was pushed back. The new teacher opened the door. He was alone.

'Hello?'

'Oh. Hi. Sorry to interrupt you . . .'

'Not at all.'

'It's just that I need the chime bars for my class.' The rather unkempt young man stood aside to let him enter and Hilary found himself unable to shut up as he edged into the tiny, overheated cell. 'It's the Junior Drama Group, you see, well more like Music and Mime really, and I get them to play co-ordination games and the chime bars make it more fun. Oh, sorry. I'm Hilary Metcalfe.'

'Rufus Barbour,' said Rufus, who had been unlocking the cupboard and now handed over an old cardboard box full of lurid blue chime bars. 'I only teach here one day a week.'

'I didn't think we'd met,' said Hilary, trying to stop the bottom from falling out of the box, 'which is odd since I've been here several months now. I see you teach little Sumitra. I do too. Is she good at the piano?'

'Not very. Her parents have nothing she can practise on.'

'Oh. Knockers.'

'Sorry?'

'I need the knocker things. I think they're in a plastic bag. Sorry.'

Rufus peered into the cupboard, pulled out the bag and carefully nestled it in the top of the box.

'Your knockers,' he said and smiled.

'Thanks.' Hilary started to go. The children would be practising some nameless horror upon poor Pat. He was also getting cramp in his hand and feeling exposed and foolish.

'Any time,' said Rufus. 'We should have a drink one evening.'

Did he say that? Did he say evening?

'But you only teach one day a week,' Hilary blurted wildly, pain searing up his forearms.

'Yes, but I thought maybe . . .' Rufus laid a hand on the door.

'Well, yes. Put a note in my pigeon-hole or something.'

'Great. Metcalfe, you said?'

'Yes.'

'You must hurry. Your bottom's falling out.'

The door was shut and the arpeggios were resumed, not so very childishly. Safe again, Hilary press-ganged a passing oaf into carrying the box, muttering darkly about a squash injury and it being well past the end of the break period.


Built as an experiment in 1970, the school's design was woefully optimistic. The staff common room, christened the *Schloss*, stood on concrete stilts in the middle of the main playground. The idea had been to place the pupils under constant protective surveillance; in practice it placed the staff under constant attack. The school functioned on a system of mutual respect in so far as the taught respected the teachers' scholastic authority on the understanding that their own terrorist authority was respected outside the prescribed instruction periods. Having dodged the catapulted turds and oh-sorry-sir footballs, each teacher seeking refuge had to scale an iron spiral staircase that came up in the heart of the *Schloss*. Once inside, one huddled near this central entrance, partly because this was where the only working gas-stove stood, partly because to sit near one of the many-windowed walls was to lose all privacy and risk at least partial maiming. When, as happened frequently, a pane was smashed, it had to be entered in the works book, together with the time of the breakage and the name of a likely vandal. Only then would the glass be replaced. Since reprisals for any meting out of justice by the staff were swift and deadly, the *Schloss*'s windows were punily webbed with sticking tape and flapping polythene.

Hilary had staggered here after showing great restraint in sending Sumitra to return the chime bars to the music block. Rachel Tuckett, the secretary, brought him a cup of cocoa. Beyond the flimsiest typing assignments, her job entailed sitting in the *Schloss* to ring the electric bells and make announcements over the tannoy between periods. She had soothed a black eye Hilary received during his second week and had unfussily mothered him ever since.

'Has Mr Barbour been a friend of yours for long?' she asked as he thanked her for the cocoa and pulled up a chair.

'Why do you ask?' Hilary discreetly eyed his pigeon-hole as he spoke.

'No reason, really. It's just that he seemed such a dark horse, only teaching one day a week, and when he brought you a note just now I thought well, that's nice; at least he's got a friend in Hilary.'

'Well, I . . .' Hilary strolled casually to the pigeon-hole and snatched out the note. 'I hardly know him.' It was written on musical manuscript paper. 'We've a few friends in common. That sort of thing.'

'So you probably know Julie.'

'Julie?'

'His girl-friend, apparently. She's Mamie Irvine's best friend.

'No, not really,' he bluffed, 'but I've heard him speak of her.'

As Rachel excused herself to ring the next bell, Hilary pulled open the note and read that he was invited to supper on Thursday. There was an address and a telephone number.

The entire episode had been one of sweet humiliation. By the time he made his way to Spanish Place on Thursday, Hilary had been wildly over-excited. The girl, Julie, had been there to start with. Absurdly pretty, she had a train to catch but had lingered so as to meet 'Rufus's new friend'. They drank beer together, then she was put in a taxi and Rufus cooked his first and only meal for Hilary. They had talked long and hard about neutral yet reassuring topics – teaching, theatre, childhood, Europe. Helping to wash up, there had been a rather more tense snatching of intimate detail, and by the time they had sat down on opposite ends of the sofa for coffee and the late news, it was clear that Rufus was not only answered for but strictly unobtainable.

Too much coffee and blended whisky, and the suspicion that – with television nearing closedown – he had already stayed unnaturally late, led Hilary to make an awkward proposition along the lines of, 'Would you ever even consider being unfaithful to Julie?'

This was rejected with a similar lack of poise and, after an interval long enough discreetly to show an incredulous host that *that* wasn't all he had come for, that they could still become friends, etcetera *etcetera*, Hilary had mounted his bicycle. He had ridden home curiously elated. After four days of groundless romantic preoccupation, he felt a wild sense of emotional liberty. The fumbling little scene had been cathartic and now he was his own master once more.

The poignancy of removing carefully chosen underwear in solitude, however, was insufferable.

Three nights later, Hilary was jolted awake in the small hours by the doorbell. There was Rufus saying words to the effect of, 'Erm . . . ah . . . I've just split up with Julie.' And there was Hilary saying words to the effect of 'What *you* need, Rufus Barbour, is some tender loving Scotch,' and here was Mr Metcalfe nearly two years on, chaining up his bicycle in the music block and thanking the Lord above for chime bars.

# Chapter Eleven

As she started to make breakfast, he had remembered that it was his day to sign on and that his UB40 was under his mattress at home. He disliked having to leave her so abruptly; from something in her manner towards him, he divined that this temporary desertion was what she desired. Naturally passive, he was perturbed by the aggression she brought out in him. As a rule sex presented a foregone conclusion of plus and minus – plus being someone else. Her behaviour challenged him to a tourney of wills. The more she had played the prying mistress, the more he had felt compelled to postures of mastery. On returning to her flat last night, he had intended to come clean, but it was as though her fantasy formed a clinging, inhibiting mould. His angry lovemaking had been a wild attempt to demonstrate his independence as she built him up into something he was not. He lacked the imagination to construct complicated fictions of mousy wives and official missions, but so palpable were her conjectures that none were needed.

'Don't you normally sign on on a Tuesday?'

Like so many of the dole clerks, this one's appearance was deceitful; close-cropped hair, earring, stubble, Nicaraguan liberation tee-shirt and doubtless – could one see – Doc Martins. The idea was to lure one into a false sense of camaraderie, to make one forget that he was not claiming illegal benefit too, but was paid a Civil Service salary.

'Yes,' said Rufus, 'but last time I came I was given a new signing day and time.'

'Are you sure of that?'

'Quite sure.'

'Because I've got you down as having missed a signing yesterday.'

'There must have been a mistake, then.' Rufus shrugged.

'You've done no work at all?' pursued the clerk.

'No. None.' He no longer blanched at the question. The sourness in the air here was enough to bring on a spasm of gagging. Rancid hair. Unwashed groin. Stale·towel.

'Well, for today you'll have to go over to that queue there, where it says "Tuesday Enquiries". Explain what's happened. They'll have your claim file.'

Rufus apologized and grunted his way through the nine queues to join the one for the most hard-bitten fraudmongers. His was an easy secret to keep. He lived alone among strangers, worked for cash and had no friends. Hilary had no suspicion, being typically naive about the cost of piano lessons, and deceived as to the extent and demands of Rufus' clientele.

Later he would lie in the bath, soaking off the sweat of the night and the smell of his fellow claimants. He would stare at his toes as they blocked off the icy draught from the overflow opening and wonder, in the state of semi-trance brought on by water that is slightly too hot, if he would be signing on for ever.

The flat – a shabbily attractive one in Spanish Place, behind the Wallace Collection – represented the chief spoil of a youthful war of charm against his maternal grandmother. Estranged from his elderly parents soon after A-levels and the first attempt on his life, he had come to lodge with her while studying music at the Guildhall School. The old woman had sustained no more than a Christmas card relationship with her daughter since an unbridled altercation over the latter's marriage, and took defiant pleasure in adopting the sole fruit of the same, never less so than when she died leaving him her property. What money remained outstanding went, in a posthumous coup, to a home for old donkeys in Kent.

Not least in the apartment's charms were its venerable Blüthner grand, and a proximity to the Wigmore Hall which, Rufus was sure, were persuasive points when advertising for pupils. While she had succumbed to electricity and a gas water-heater over the bath, his grandmother had held out staunchly against the conspiracies of central heating and Alexander Bell. A gas-fire provided the sole source of warmth, and there was a payphone in the hall which Rufus shared with visitors to the parsimonious freeholder who lived on the ground floor. He had never redecorated the place. The walls had faded to a pleasing antique cream and were still hung with the inferior paintings amassed by the old woman and her late banker husband. The oil of these had darkened with age, abstracting their sentimental subjects further with each passing year. Rufus' influence was shown only in small ways: a frying-pan permanently on the stove, the removal of all net curtains, and the contemporary fiction which gradually ousted her collected editions of Walter Scott, Dumas *fils* and Angela Thirkell. When in especially dire financial straits, he would carry another handful of her books to a nearby dealer. He had left untouched his grandmother's drapes over the bed: a baroque confection of gilt hoops and dusty silk which amused him. When disturbed, these hangings gave off a smell instantly recognizable by anyone who has ever emptied the wastepaper basket in their grandmother's bedroom; and evocative blend of nylon stocking, hair spray and slightly stale scent. Rufus often reflected, not without a little sadness, that he would appreciate his grandmother more now than in the unlovely years of his late adolescent preoccupation.

Dry now, smelling faintly of baby powder, he wandered naked in search of clothes. His grandmother's pride and joy had been a full-length looking glass given her on her twentieth birthday, which she had arranged so as to multiply her severe reflection in a second glass built into a tallboy door. An arching infinity of grandsons now crouched to a plastic basket of clean boxer shorts, now stood on tip-toe to select a well-ironed shirt. While not of theatrical proportions, his wardrobe was unconsciously assembled an outfit at a time, each ensemble so different from the last as to present a second, seventh, sixteenth character. For Mrs Phillips, the army wife, he dressed down in jeans but with a good jacket to show that he could dress up should the need arise. For the brats at school he dressed as wholesome youth – deck shoes, bright shirt, soft jersey. He dressed for Gibley as for a prince – his best suit, Hilditch and Key shirting, an

60

exquisite tie an Italian friend had once left behind.

Gavin Gibley was twelve. His mother had evidently booked him in with Rufus under some misapprehension. Every week the mournfully talentless child was let off school for the morning to be dressed in his best flannel suit and clip-on bow tie, and put on the bus from Mill Hill. Gibley would be here in twenty minutes. As he walked his way into his best shoes, Rufus set a bowl of potpourri on the piano; Gibley reeked of piss.

Rufus dabbed on his strongest cologne as further protection, adjusted the stool and launched into his scales. He would never be a soloist, but he would never admit the same by letting his standards slip. When he made a mistake he barely frowned, but briefly withdrew his hands, paused for recollection and then returned to the beginning of the blemished run. The gamut of scales complete, he stretched, then took down a book of masochistic but effective nineteenth-century studies. He chose the twenty-fifth. *For the Development of the Power in the Fifth Fingers, and a Facility in Hand-crossing.*

Clinically examined, the Metcalfe affair could be seen as an out-of-hand experiment. Hilary was the only man with whom he had ever, could ever have been involved. When they first met he had been perfectly happy with a Canadian flautist from Guildhall called Julie who was blonde and absurdly pretty. She was also successful. His only professional engagements since leaving college had been as her accompanist at three lunchtime concerts in the Barbican foyer.

'Invite him round, why don't you?' she had suggested when he told her about the young, lonely-seeming teacher encountered at school. 'I'm off for the weekend, but you could cook him your lasagne. You need some friends of your own.'

With the arrogance natural in the perennially popular, she had always assumed that his marked lack of acquaintance was due to some fault, rather than any desire on his part. He understood this and let her pity him accordingly. Though he had already invited Hilary Metcalfe, he let her assume that he now did so at her behest. She stayed long enough to patronize the happy spectacle of 'Rufus making friends', then swanned off, quite lovely, to Victoria.

The amusing thing was that as the evening drew on, he

found that he really was making friends. With ingenuous brutality, Hilary clambered into his closest chested concerns – asking politely about his parents, then their rift with his grandmother, then his rift with them and on to his ambitions and the slowness of getting his career off the ground. Once he started to confide it was surprisingly easy, but with each unbuttoning came a stab of panic as this young stranger calmly opened another pocket of his history. Hilary had confided in his turn and reversed the process, which was still more alarming. The confessions of his failure in love, his lack of professional motivation and his undying romantic optimism trapped Rufus as firmly as if his guest had been repeatedly seizing him by the hand and pressing his fingers on portions of a wounded anatomy.

'Feel here,' he was demanding. 'And here. Look. Touch. Feel the damage.'

The thinly masked suggestion that they make love was the logical conclusion to a conversation that could only become increasingly personal. Although Rufus refused, with the instinctive flinching which could subsequently be shrugged off as disgust, he could register no convincing astonishment. When Hilary released him by riding away, Rufus had felt the high-charged guilt appropriate to a conceptual adultery.

'Hi there,' Julie laughed after she had pushed him on to the sofa and kissed him thoroughly as a reward for being a good boy all solitary weekend. 'And how was your new friend?'

'Fine,' he told her. 'We made love.'

She failed to understand. He had always been most accommodating when she buried her shame in his shoulder and stuttered out the latest peccadillo, but it seemed that the rules were different for him. He said as much to her telephone answering machine, trying to make her see that she was being unreasonable. He went around to her flat and made a shortish speech into her entryphone on the subject of conjugal equality and rational behaviour.

'It wasn't as though I'd fooled around with another woman,' he told her, but she seemed to think it was worse. On reflection, guilty in thought if not yet in deed, he was inclined to agree with her. After twenty-four hours of exhausting theory, he had caught the first of many taxis to the North Pole and claimed the late-night practice that seemed by now to be his due.

The study ended with a frivolous flourish, banal after the dogged hard work of the previous three pages. He shook the tensions from his hands, rubbed his palms on his trouser legs and took out a Debussy prelude. *Feuilles Mortes*.

Doubtless Hilary analysed the painful scenes of several months past and decided with characteristic Broadway ham humility that he was being punished for being over-affectionate. This was not the case. Rufus needed all or nothing; smothering or total liberty. If Hilary had turned up one day with a car instead of that ridiculous bicycle and said, 'We're going to a cottage in Drumnadrochit and never coming back,' he would have leapt in beside him. It was Hilary's hesitation that did the damage, the self-effacing guilt he felt for showing affection. If he pulled back, Rufus pulled back also. If he tried not to sit up waiting, Rufus felt compelled to oblige him by not being there for breakfast the next morning. Hilary assumed that Rufus had a promiscuous appetite for other men and here he did himself a gross injustice. He was and would ever be the only man in Rufus' life.

Half-way through he was interrupted by the doorbell. He hurled a damp towel into the bathroom and loped down to the hall. In a new sky-blue bow-tie, Gibley waited on the doorstep, joyless and sulphurous as ever.

'Hello,' said Gibley.

'Hello, Gavin,' said Rufus and they walked upstairs. Rufus took his coat and hung it on the hatstand. 'Coffee? A glass of milk?'

'No, thank you.' Nothing was ever seen to pass Gibley's lips. Were it not for the smell, the boy could be an android.

'Sure?'

'Yes, thank you.'

Gibley had sat down and was solemnly adjusting the height of the piano stool so that his feet could reach the pedals.

'Right then,' said Rufus once he had finished. 'Let's hear your scales. E flat major and D sharp minor this week, wasn't it?'

'That's right.'

'Off you go then.'

Off went Gibley. Rufus stood behind him and stared down to the street where two cats were failing to couple on the soft top of a Jaguar.

The medical officer at Bishop Chandler's School for Boys had relieved him of his virginity while tending a rugby injury. He had reported the incident and she had abruptly left the staff. Sandy had the same hands. For that matter, so did Hilary. Rufus turned.

'No. Look. Stop,' he said. Gibley stopped.

'What?' said Gibley.

'You're bringing your thumb under as though it was a club foot. It should happen smoothly, otherwise you'll be in real trouble when you try to speed it up. Let me show you.'

He pushed Gibley lightly on the shoulder and took his place on the piano stool. As he ran his fingers back and forth over the same six notes to demonstrate a smoother thumb action, he decided to see Hilary tonight instead of Sandy. Evenings with Hilary were fraught, but they were oddly necessary.

# Chapter Twelve

It was already dark as Henry trudged across the central courtyard where the cars were parked. The slushed snow had frozen into rocky ridges and a cruel wind was whipping fresh flakes into her face and hair. As she burrowed in her bag to find the key, someone thrust a revolver into the small of her back and a man's voice said, 'Open the passenger door first, then drive me to Chester Square.'

She froze, one hand still in the depths of her bag and, with just the tip of her thumb, pressed her radio alarm.

'That's not a gun,' she said. 'It's a piece of hot-water piping and we both know that if you hit me over the head and steal the car you won't get past the gates.' The piping was jerked hard into her back. She gasped and bit her upper lip.

'Unlock the door,' the man repeated. There was a faint Lancashire accent. She failed to recognize the voice, which could mean that he was a high security patient who had still to be relocated. She was breathing fast and shallowly.

'I won't scream,' she said in a low voice. 'I won't try to run away. Just drop the piping so that I can trust you, then I'll let you into the car and we can talk.' The piping remained against her spine. 'Go on,' she urged, wishing there was someone else in the courtyard. 'I promise I won't snatch it.'

'I'm a fool. That's what I am, a fucking fool,' he said and she heard the piping fall. It fell surprisingly heavily.

She sighed and unlocked her door. Without turning she said, 'Go round. I'll let you in,' and climbed inside, shutting the door beside her. She could have driven away at once, but she was so relieved that he had done as she asked, and his voice had sounded so apologetic that she lifted the catch on the passenger door and opened it. He sat beside her, breathing rapidly. The yard was ill-lit and she could see only his profile, black against the great, glaring kitchen windows several yards away. Suddenly he turned with an impatient smack of hand on knee.

'Just drive, won't you, woman?'

'Where to?'

'I told you just now; Chester Square.'

'Why there?'

'There's no time to explain. Just drive, for fuck's sake, and I'll talk as we go along.'

The ignition key stayed unturned in its slot. She rested her hands on the worn suede of the wheel cover.

'Not unless you tell me why you're so frightened.'

'Please hurry. They'll be on to me soon, you little git. It's the third time I've tried.'

'I'm Dr Metcalfe,' she said. 'I think I can help you if you'll just talk.'

'Fuck off.'

'Fuck off yourself.'

He grabbed the lapels of her overcoat and shook her. Her hands flew to his wrists and found them thick with muscle and vein.

'I'm not ill.' His terror was hot on her face. 'I'm here under false pretences. I'm as sane as you, probably saner.'

'Then why are you here? What motive could anyone have for sending you?'

'I cheated them. For three years I was signing on as unemployed. They paid me supplementary benefit, housing benefit, heating allowance, child allowance, my wife and two children had free dental treatment, I had free glasses, the kids had free milk and all the bleeding while,' here he shook her again for emphasis, 'I was raking in a small fortune as a fixer.'

'What's that?'

'Boilers, windows, cars – anything wrong, they'd call me and I'd come round and fix it for them. Cash in hand. No questions asked. Then someone grassed on me. They spied on my wife to make sure we were living together. They followed my children to school to watch how much they spent on sweets. Eventually they started following me. I tried to protect us. We drove to London and rented a flat. I nailed up the windows and put extra chains on the door but . . .' He seemed about to weep. 'They brought me here just the same.'

His grip on her lapels had weakened. Gently she lifted his hands off and lowered them, wrapped in hers, to her lap.

'Look,' she said, 'I sounded the alarm when you attacked me because I didn't know who you were. Now that I do, I can send them away. Stay here.' So saying, she started to open the door.

'Don't leave me,' he whimpered. 'They'll give me electric shock treatment.'

'It's OK,' she said, hating her well-worn sincerity of tone. 'Trust me.'

His head sank forward and she opened her door. As she stepped out, one of her feet struck something heavy on the ice. She glanced down and saw a revolver gleaming against the snow. She closed the door behind her and strode in the direction of the advancing orderlies.

'The door's unlocked,' she said, then stood warming herself by the kitchen windows. They took him, uncomplaining, away. As she climbed back into her seat, she slipped the revolver behind the 1972 AA manual in the glove compartment. Then she began to shake.

# Chapter Thirteen

The classroom was thick with the fug of damp wool and hot child. 15B was one of the smaller forms – thirty-eight pupils on the rare days without absenteeism – and was littered with empty desks. *Shri Metcalfe* encouraged them to spread out. It was less intimidating for him than a tight phalanx in the first few rows, and hindered cheating, terrorism and the passing-round of horrors.

Sumitra sat at the back in isolation. No one had ever offered to sit by her and she gave no invitations. Of the three Asians in the room, she was the only Hindu and the sole girl. The Muslims sat at the front. She stank, they opined, like rotten pig. Her Anglo-Saxon classmates had been quick to brand her 'Sue' to deflate her exotic difference and so render her defenceless as any other twelve-year-old. Her quick mind had landed her in a class a year older than herself so that her slight form, sunk in the tomb-dark desk, was dwarfed by Tamsin, Kerry and the rest. Her legs, dressed at her father's insistence in boy's black polyester trousers, itched as they swung. Her spotless hands lay palms down on the wood as she stared across at her god.

Overnight the prophecies had come true. As he paced the dais, discussing the dire effects of blood upon the guilty mind, pausing occasionally to cough or run a perfect hand through his dirty-blond hair, she thrilled to the thought of last night's nativity. She had sensed that something was afoot when the music continued so late. He lived on the first floor of the main body of the house, so she could just see his windows from her own. As self-elected handmaid to the Word, she never rested

68

until she could peer up from her bed over the chest freezers and see his light extinguished. Last night the light had burned, the music had continued until well after twelve. It had also started to snow, which tied in precisely with her prophetic dreams and the pictures in the shrine. Perhaps two hours after his light went out, she had leapt awake, certain she had heard a new baby's cry. In the silence that followed she had convinced herself it was a dream, but the night proved restless. Repeatedly she had woken to lie watching down on the freezers' green lights, her mind dwelling on the idea of his pain, her ears prickling in anticipation of further aural proof. Did gods bleed? Had he suffered greatly? Had he – perish the unworthy thought – died in labour?

Washing before *puja*, she had glanced up to his bathroom window and been stunned. He was standing, quite naked, cradling a freshly-swaddled baby in his tender arms. Furthermore, the baby had been of her own race.

The god had realized his perfection on earth. He was now *Narendra Saraswati*. Prince Goddess. All human potential in one body. But still her frail faith required a sign.

His back was turned as he drew a diagram on the board. 'Letter' arrow 'Welcome' arrow 'Duncan' arrow 'Murder' arrow 'Coronation' arrow. He continued to write. Kerry passed a lewd sketch to Tamsin, who had to stick out her tongue in an effort not to laugh. Sumitra quickly tore a sheet from her notepad, scribbled across it 'Sumitra 4 *Shri Metcalfe, Narendra Saraswati*' and stuffed it in her mouth. Now he drew a vertical line from the left-hand corner of the progression of words and arrows and, switching to blue chalk, wrote 'Marital Estrangement' beside it.

'What's "marital" mean, sir?' asked Josette, a skinny thing with blue patches in her cheeks.

'Having to do with marriage. Love, trust and sex basically,' he said without turning. There was an explosive titter, although no one had found this especially funny. Sumitra chewed desperately, reducing the mulch to a damp, hard pellet which she then rolled between her palms. 'Hysterical really,' he said slowly, concentrating on drawing an unsteady diagonal to illustrate that the more one eggs him on to murder and ambition, the less attractive one's husband is likely to find one.

'And now, while you all copy this down, I'll hand back those essays. Fairly dreadful for the most part. Tomorrow – no, it's the day after that I see you next, isn't it? Yes? Well, the day after tomorrow we'll have a crash course on "How to Write Essays".' He started to walk amongst the desks, tossing books to owners. If she could only swallow the pellet in time, she should have a sign. Straining her tongue, she forced it to the back of her mouth. The ink was bitter. She hoped her lips were not blue. 'Fair, er, Duncan. Fair. Not bad, Tracey. Wayne, see me. Tony, see me. Er . . .' He forgot a Muslim's name. 'Yes. See me.' The book was hastily tossed. 'Mandy, awful.' Mandy grimaced. 'Tamsin and Kerry, I know the value of friendship, but team work is frowned on by examiners. I've shared your mark between you. One essay each next time, please. Sumitra? Ah, there you are.' He turned and strode to her desk. Kerry giggled. Sumitra swallowed violently and the pellet ground its way down her throat. She parted her lips, unable to smile. Her book had fallen shut. He opened it to remind himself of his comments, then smiled and tossed it to her. She missed her catch and had to scrabble on the floor for the prize. He returned to the dais. 'I was wrong,' he said. 'Not all the essays were awful; Sumitra's was excellent. She's a year younger than you and English is her third language. Since half of you can barely order breakfast in French, I hope that puts you all to shame.'

A sign! His earthly powers in fruit, he had now acknowledged his handmaid. Sumitra dug a nail into her forearm to stop herself from grinning. Tamsin was holding a paper behind her back which read, 'Sue is a Pakki slimer.'

'Tonight you can draw another graph like this one,' he went on, 'to illustrate the fall and rise (or is it rise and fall?) of the powers of good against the play's career of evil. Also – and this is more important, Scott, thank you – I want you all to learn Lady M's first speech by heart.' There were groans all round. 'Not much. Just from the end of Macbeth's letter to his entry on the next page,' he countered. 'Only a few lines. You'll be grateful for them in the exams. Now, who did I ask to come and see me?'

He had finished early. His preoccupation was forgivable. Not every man gives birth on his own, without a nurse's hands or grandmother's comfort, and is still able to come to work the next day. Still pondering on the marvel that was her parents' tenant, Sumitra followed the back of the crowd as it barged into the corridor and hurried towards the yard. She took a different turning and sprinted to the locker room. It was empty. She reached inside her shirt and pulled out a key tied round her neck by a string. Making doubly sure she was unobserved, she kissed the key and unfastened the padlock on her locker door.

On the outside it was no different from the others; a square wooden door, eighteen by eighteen. There the resemblance ceased. The inside was lined with cooking foil, pinned up with extreme care so as to keep the surface as wrinkle-free as possible. A bowl of spiced, dried flowers gave off a rich, musky odour. Behind it, in a plastic gilt frame stolen from her father's store, stood a photograph of the *Narendra Saraswati*. His friend, the muscular, dark-haired one who gave her piano lessons, had let it fall when hurrying out of the house once. She had snatched it up. It was her greatest treasure. In it the *Narendra* was leaning against a tree, his arms folded, his shoulders dappled with sunlight through the leaves. He was smiling, his face less burdened with the cares of godhead than it was now. On the back some writing was pressed by a rubber stamp. *Starbright Agency* – returned with thanks. This added greatly to the relic's power. In the prayer hall that she visited with her parents, there were no photographs of Rama and Sita, only crude paintings and ugly ceremonial dolls.

The two side walls were adorned with a collage of images cut from the cards left around school before the festival they called Xmas. Babies in well-lined cribs. Stars. Angels. Smirking ox and sentimental ass. The virgins' heads she had cut off and replaced with heads of male models in colour magazines. She dared not cut up her only photograph of the *Narendra*, and these served as stereotypical approximations of his loveliness.

Sumitra touched her forehead and bowed slightly in greeting; then, taking out a pair of embroidery scissors shaped like a stork, she opened her English book and carefully cut out the paper bearing the *Narendra*'s glowing praise of her essay. She replaced the scissors, took out a drawing pin and fixed the lines to the door beside other, lesser samples of his handwriting, including last term's report and a discarded envelope he had addressed to a man who shared his name and lived in Paris. Finally she lifted the small saucer of Smarties set before the Presence, muttered a few suitable words, then slipped the sweets into her mouth. Before she locked the door once more, she restocked the votive saucer, this time with Dolly Mixture. She had learnt that variety in her domestic pilfering was good insurance against detection.

As she slipped the keys back beneath her shirt, a gym class finished and the room was a bruising mass of gross white legs and arms. She skidded out, sheltering her face from injury and went her way.

# Chapter Fourteen

Hilary met Mrs Sharma in the hall as he opened the door. He started to say hello but she silenced him, pressing a finger to her lips and then pointing to the ceiling with such a broad smile that he wondered if she were not quite herself. With much gesticulating, and almost touching his arm, she let herself out. He dropped his briefcase at the bottom of the stairs, for it was one of the few nights of the week free of marking, and padded upstairs, snow-sodden shoes in hand.

In marked contrast to his sister, Hilary tended to surround himself with objects. His impulse to collect was eclectic as a wealthy Texan's and he had a twelve-year-old's reluctance to throw things away. His flat, which took up the top floor, while the Sharmas spread through various extensions around the shop below, was cluttered with photographs, china and magazine racks. Miscellanea which had amused him from junkshop windows or market stalls were borne proudly home to find their niche in the companionable magpie nest. What to his sister's eye represented a nightmare of interior design, however, had for him the precision, the 'rightness' of an ever-growing personal mosaic. In his absence, Dan had taken over the living room. The carrycot stood empty in a corner with a folded-up pushchair. What books remained on the desk had been stacked up to make space for a gaudy changing mat. Two packets of disposable nappies lay in the armchair; a third lay opened on the desk. Dan's feeding bottle was soaking, dismantled, in sterilizing fluid. The top left drawer of the chest of drawers was pulled open and filled with carefully folded babygros, hats, bootees, disarmingly midget gloves joined with elastic, and an assortment of dwarf jerseys in various pastel shades. On the back of the door an efficient-looking anorak was hooked up, like the lagging for a Toytown boiler. Even by Hilary's lumber-room standards, his home looked more than slightly bombed.

The first cause of all this transformation lay, breathing deeply as ever, in an imposing blue cot in the corner where Hilary usually dragged a square of hardboard on which to practise his tap dancing. Hilary sat on the sofa and peered closely at him. Beyond question he was extremely attractive, probably clever, at present defenceless and decidedly domineering. Hilary reached a finger through the bars and stroked the back of one of Daniel's hands.

'What are you *doing* here?' he whispered. The telephone rang and he snatched it up before a second ring could wake the baby. 'Hello?' he whispered.

'Hil?'

'Richard. Hi.'

'Why are you whispering?'

'Long story. Thanks for a lovely evening.'

'Not at all.'

'What are you doing tonight?'

'I was meant to be dragging you to your dance class, remember?'

'Oh God, Rich, I can't.'

'Why not?'

Dan was making waking noises. Hilary threw him a rapid glance.

'I just can't. All right?'

'Fine. I won't ask. Give him my modified love.'

'No. It's not . . .'

'Happy birthday, Hil. Speak to you soon.'

'I'm sorry.'

'Why *are* you whispering?'

''Bye.'

'Be like that.'

Richard and Hilary had both taken their acting seriously from the start, although Richard had veered more towards the

74

Shakespearean, his friend towards the 'French Window' school. Now Richard had an Equity card and was playing Lady MacDuff in a Kabuki Macbeth in a pub theatre, while paying his rent by appearing several times nightly on three channels in a mattress commercial. The one dramatic form in the ascendant at the moment was the musical. Revivals of inanities from 1920 and every decade since frolicked across West End stages, leaving blank verse to the converted churches and Richard to sign autographs for being 'The Slumbersoftie Man', muttering darkly the while about a cultural winter. Hilary had procured his Equity card through a friend of his father's but, disheartened by a set of dismal auditions, had taken on his teaching post out of greed. The original idea, as professed to Richard and a cynical friend Bridget, had been to regard teaching solely as a cash fund and to have no qualms about taking days off whenever a good audition came along. Things had turned out slightly differently, as had the dance classes. To be in shape for an audition he would have to go to classes at least every other night, and to limber up at home every day. In practice he rarely had the energy to ride down to Hammersmith after a day's work, and his home work-outs had dwindled to an occasional bout in his tap shoes on the square of hardboard, with Geoff Bernardi and the Boomtown Tappers Band on the gramophone. Though a 'serious' actor, Richard had pledged himself to the jazz dance classes to give his friend moral support.

Dan moved his head slightly and yawned without truly waking. Hilary found himself an apple and a glass of milk in the kitchen and then returned, munching, to the telephone. Lying on the sofa, his socked toes rubbing on the bars of the cot, he dialled a familiar number. Rufus answered almost at once.

'Rufus?'

'Hi, Sandy. How did you . . .?'

'Rufus, it's Hilary. Who's Sandy?'

There was a delay at the other end, then Rufus answered in a rush.

'Hello, Hil. Sorry, Sandy's just arrived. She's a pupil.'

'Oh. Right.'

'Why are you whispering?'

'Sore throat. Can we talk?'

'Yes. She's . . . erm . . . she's in the bathroom.'

'How are you?'

'Fine.'

'Sorry I wasn't in last night, I'd . . .'

'Well, I'm sorry I didn't make it. You see . . .'

They had both spoken at once; now there was a silence which each waited for the other to break. Hilary took the initiative.

'Roof, you can't come round here tonight.'

'Why not?'

'Well . . . you see.' He couldn't tell him about Dan; Rufus loathed babies. 'Oh, Christ, it's sheer chaos. Mrs Sharma's got relatives staying and I let her put one of the children to sleep up here.'

'Well, that was stupid of you. Where will you . . .'

'Well, I thought perhaps I could come over to you for once. We haven't seen each other for nearly a week and I thought we could go out and . . .'

'I told you,' Rufus' tone was weary. 'Sandy's just arrived. I'll be teaching her until nearly half seven.'

'Well, I wouldn't come over until . . .'

'Look, Hil, this is stupid. It's no accident that we haven't seen each other in a week. It's more than a week, in fact. Look, I . . . Why don't we just let it go?'

'Let it go?' Hilary became aware that he was holding the half-eaten apple hard against his cheek. As he raised his voice, Dan started to wake in earnest.

'Yes. I mean, you're out teaching all day there, and I teach all day here and . . . well. Just let's let it go, OK?'

'But I thought you said . . .'

'I've got to go now. Sandy's waiting.'

'Sandy who?'

'Grow up.'

'Thanks.'

'Look. It didn't work. You could do better for yourself. OK?' This didn't seem either real or fair.

'It isn't OK. I'll write to you.'

'What?' Rufus sounded bored. Hilary's voice trailed off as

he reiterated, 'Could I write to you?'
Rufus hung up.


Hilary took several aggressive bites to finish his apple. Dan
gurgled. Hilary stood and ran to the kitchen. He rinsed out the
bottle, made up some milk and came back. Without flinching,
he felt Dan's bum and was rewarded by finding it dry.
'Wonderbaby!' he exclaimed and lifted the boy on to his lap.
He found that if he sat in the left-hand corner of the sofa and
leaned Dan in the crook of his left arm, he could feed him with
his left hand, so leaving his right hand free. He chewed most of
his apple core, then threw the fibrous rest into the bin. He
stared dreamily at his borrowed son. As Dan fed, he fluffed up
the child's hair where the sweat of sleep had plastered it to his
forehead. 'Do you love me, mmm?' he asked. 'No? Not yet?
Well, you should.' He tapped the crocus bulb nose with his
forefinger. Dan stared at him agape and hiccoughed, then
returned to his milk.


So . . . they were to let it go. There was little left to release.
Love, Hilary reflected, was now largely force of habit. Love, in
their case, had dwindled to making enough spaghetti sauce for
two in case someone turned up. Love was having somebody to
worry about besides oneself. Not very poetic really. Not much
to miss.
'The trouble with you,' Rufus had once mocked, 'is your
pathological inability to separate sex from domesticity.'
This was true, Hilary knew, but Rufus's values were plain
unnatural. Everyone needed domesticity. One had to have a
home – food, at least – and a roof. A roof. Most amusing.
While Hilary could not be called frigid, he did find passion less
vital than comfort. He had often winced with guilt to hear
himself cool Rufus' advances in favour of something less
strenuous. On the last occasion when he and Bridget had
played word association, she had said 'Men' and he had
answered, 'Breakfast'. While breakfast in bed was, in a sense, a
treat to compensate for the lack of sleep, he now wondered
whether the treat would feel as special if it had not been

earned. The telephone rang again and Dan watched, fascinated, as he answered.

'Hello?'

'Hi. I feel ghastly! I forgot your birthday.' It was Evelyn Peake, his godmother.

'Hello, Evelyn. It doesn't matter. Honestly.'

'At least, I bought you a card, but I clean forgot to send it. Will you come to tea and tell me all your news?'

'Lovely. How about tomorrow? I finish early.'

'Marvellous. Three-thirtyish?'

'Can't wait. I've got a baby on my lap, by the way.'

'Goodness. Whose?'

'Well, it seems to be mine for the moment.'

'But Hilary, that's absolutely wonderful,' Evelyn enthused, scenting a cause. 'You mean you've adopted it?'

'I just found him.'

'What a superb idea! We must talk it over tomorrow. I've got to fly; there's someone at the door and Bids is barking the house down.'

'OK. 'Bye. And thanks.'

He replaced the receiver. There was a dull thump against a window-pane. He glanced up in time to see a snowball sliding down the glass.

'Oi,' Henry called from the street. 'I think your doorbell's bust again and I'm cold.'

He should have told her about the baby. She would never understand at short notice.

'Coming,' he yelled. He tried to make Dan lie down, but the latter protested so loudly that he had to hurry downstairs, comforting him against a shoulder. He opened the door. 'Sorry.'

Her overcoat had snow on the shoulders. Her cheeks were pink and taut. She looked well. She shuddered theatrically and pushed past him into the warmth. As he closed the door she started up the stairs, calling over her shoulder,

'Looking after the landlord's babies now, are we?'

'Well, not exactly.'

He was about to explain that, actually, it was the other way around, but she forestalled him, coming to an abrupt standstill in the living-room doorway.

'Oh my *God*! Hilary, what's happened?'

'Sit down.' He motioned her to the sofa. He could see that she was all prepared to lecture him. Whenever they met she was ready to be all loving and sisterly, but he always seemed to do or say something wrong within minutes of her arrival. 'It's absurd really,' he began, 'but I found him in the subway last night. Well, obviously I couldn't just leave him there to die of exposure, and it was too late and I was too tired to go calling out the police, so I brought him home. I marched him round to the local clinic this morning to hand him over, as it were, and they said oh no, I had to keep him until they could arrange an adoption.'

'But that's mad.' Henry laughed. 'They can't expect you to . . .'

'I was only trying to be a good Samaritan, and they ended up making out I was trying to dump my bastard on them.' He sat with Dan on the arm of the sofa, laughing back at her. She was taking it better than he had supposed. Perhaps he would tell her about Rufus. 'Anyway,' he continued, 'I was in a dreadful rush for school and by the time they'd finished with me I felt so guilty I thought I might as well.'

'Might as well what?' The warning note came back to her voice.

'Look after him for a bit. Mrs Sharma's lent me all this stuff, very sweetly, and says she'll mind him during the day. He's no trouble. Just sleeps and needs feeding and changing occasionally.'

'Changing?'

'Nappies.'

'Oh.' Henry raised her eyebrows and looked faintly disgusted. 'Could I have a drink, Hil? It's been a *vile* day.'

'Yup. Wine?'

'Great.'

'Hold this, then.'

He handed Dan to her unwelcoming arms, noticing for the first time that she didn't have much in the way of a lap, and went to the kitchen for some wine. She called out after him, 'Hang on, Hil. I don't know what I'm saying. No, of course I can't have any wine. I must rush.'

'Oh. Can't you stay for supper?' He came back and found

79

her standing holding Dan the wrong way, with his head askew. He rescued the child.

'No. It's very kind of you but I'm expecting someone.'

'That's nice. Anyone I know?'

'No. He's a friend from work, really,' she lied.

'Oh, I see. That sort of friend.'

'But this is all absurd.' She waved a hand at *this*, who was kneading Hilary's chest. 'We must do something. I'll make some calls tomorrow and get him taken away for you.'

'Well, if you think . . . but wouldn't it be better if . . .?'

'Hil, you can't let them bully you like that. Honestly, I ought to file a complaint. Thinking a boy could look after a newborn baby!'

'I'm twenty-five.'

'Oh shit. So you are. And I have got a present, but it's at home. I'll drop it round, all right?'

'OK.'

She started for the stairs.

'Oh yes. Before you go, you couldn't possibly do me a sick note for school?'

'Yes. Fine,' she sighed and pulled out her notepad. 'How long for?'

'Just this morning.'

'Food poisoning suit you? Sounds likely enough after a birthday.'

'Great,' he said as she scribbled. 'Thanks. Dad rang, by the way. Sent you his love.'

'Good.' She gave him the note.

'Sorry you can't stay.'

'So am I.' She pulled on her coat. 'But you know . . . Are you at home tomorrow morning?'

'Only till nine-fifteen.'

'Fine. I'll get someone round. 'Bye.'

She kissed him briskly on the cheek and was gone.


Hilary opened his briefcase and took out the baby bath and powder he had bought on the way home. Upstairs he held his fingers under the water; waiting for it to run hot, he felt faint but distinct stirrings of fraternal rebellion. In the living room the telephone rang again.

# Chapter Fifteen

'Pour boiling water over sachet and leave to stand for thirty seconds,' Henry muttered as she read the instructions on the packet. She rinsed the coffee grounds out of a mug and threw in the sachet, then poured on boiling water from the kettle and sat on the kitchen stool to eye the second hand of her watch. Beneath her towel, her body glowed pink from a zealous session with some Naturegrains Bodyscrub in the bath. 'Eliminates that grey, tired look by sloughing off dead cell layer and skin impurities' the packet had promised. The stuff had been unexpectedly mentholated, so as well as having a raw thigh, she smelt like a bag of lightly toasted mint imperials. Twenty-eight, twenty-nine, thirty. She tipped out the coffeeish water and chased the sachet like a spiteful goldfish around the sink, burning her fingers. 'Snip off corner and spread liberally over damp hair,' she read. The scissors were not in evidence, so she used the bread knife and then spread the lurid oil over her hair. The Luvlox Hairpak was evidently designed for waist-length tresses, for it overran her boyish crop, coursing stickily down her spine. 'Wrap in hot towel and relax for fifteen minutes.' Tugging the towel from her body and winding it in a precarious turban over her unpleasantly squelching scalp. She left the kitchen and sat, naked, on the chaise-longue.

A steady rain was falling now, puckering the river face and clouding her view of the other bank. Occasional slabs of melting snow slithered off the roof and past her balcony. She stared, remorsefully unconvinced, at her exotic reflection.

Someone had mended the telephone line during the day. There had been a message on the answering machine (given her by Dad several Christmases ago) from Candy asking her to supper, and one from Marie-Claude to say that she would try again tomorrow. Ignoring Candy, Henry had tried to ring her parents, but found them out.

The visit to Hilary had been abortive too. Whenever she mentioned him to friends, she saw that they pictured a snug alliance. My brother. Hugs. Loyal affection. Midnight analyses. Fond reminiscence. Indeed, all this had been there until he went away to Durham, when suddenly she had found it harder. He loved men, of course, but if anything that should have fostered the same sisterly kinship she felt for M–C. They had raised a barrier of cowardly silence on the subject, however, which was foolish. It was not that she disapproved. Rather, she had no feelings one way or the other.

As she drove to North Pole Road this evening, still shaken from her encounter in the hospital car park, she had imagined bursting into his bachelor den with cakes and kisses. She would tease him about being a twenty-five-year-old chorus boy, and he would tease her for being considerably older and single, then they would laugh and fall on the sofa and . . . and she would tell him all about being held at gunpoint by a patient. Then perhaps, just perhaps, she would tell him about her new man and how she was actually being Someone's Mistress. Then maybe he would come clean and tell her about the special person in his life and maybe the person would turn up and they could all do something lazily comfortable like eat beans on toast by the telly. But the cake shop had been closed. And his doorbell hadn't worked. And when she did get in, she couldn't kiss him because he had an armful of baby.

That baby! She couldn't cope with that baby. He had always seemed *sadly* single – in contrast to her voluntary, intermittent spinsterhood – but then, he had always kept his private life from her view. Since her first visit to his digs in the cottage at Durham, he had presented a seamless front of bachelor domesticity: tea, toast and neutral conversation. From the moment she saw all those baby things in his living room, she had sensed that he had no intention of letting the thing go. Whatever he said, professional intuition told her that he wanted to be a single father. He even knew how to hold the creature properly. She had had to rush home because of her shock at the spite which suddenly boiled up inside her. Without the baby she could look on him as satisfactorily failed – not even an academic, but a low-flying teacher who wanted to be a chorus boy; now he made her feel as selfish as did those women one was always hearing on the radio, the ones who left work to go on the dole and adopt unwanted spastics. Even though she had devoted her teens to his welfare, she could see that he was the one who would end up appearing sacrificial. If he had his way, that was. Driving home, she had determined to have the child taken away. It was not as though she was jealous. She had never wanted a baby herself; being a surrogate mother at the tender age of ten had cauterized all such impulses. As she lolled, at once nude and orientally adorned, her wry reflection was that her proper reaction under the circumstances should be that of a smug new grandmother.

Stupid of her to forget his present. She had bought him the new Richard Rodgers biography. The shop had wrapped it for her. She could see it on the bread-bin now. It had cost the earth, but it was exactly what he wanted.

Fifteen minutes up, Henry rinsed out the Hairpak under the kitchen tap then towelled her hair dry. It had worked; her thin, blonde crop felt full and soft. She brushed it back off her face with a little gel, staring narrowly in the mirror. She liked it tight back like that; she fancied it made her look like a smart, enigmatically lesbian sportswoman. She never wore make-up, but she had her eyelashes dyed dark brown. She pulled on a favourite black dress; a knee-length silk affair that showed her thin legs to advantage and made her feel like an expensive fountain pen.

She was glad now that she hadn't told Hilary about Andrew. She would have loved to see the surprise on his face, and it might have made her less of a bossy elder sister in his eyes, but his condescension would have been inevitable. After she had left, he would have felt sorry for her, imagining that her lover was bound to return to his wife in the end, leaving her with nothing. He would cast her in the role of the career woman intellectual of magazine mythology, whose private life never gets off the ground because she's not prepared to make the slightest compromise to her emotions.

*Would* he leave her with nothing and go back to his wife?

83

Probably. But then, he would leave her with nothing but memories of an adventure, which was all she wanted. She had decided long ago that she could not afford to want anything more. Hadn't she? Oh God.

Henry·poured herself a Martini cocktail. She had made up a batch in a jug in her fridge, because this seemed the sort of thing that Sandy would do. She tossed a stuffed olive into her mouth, dropped a second one into the glass and walked back to the chaise-longue to wait.

Why was she waiting? He hadn't rung and they had nothing arranged. He had said he would come, but it was more likely that he was watching home videos with a wife and 2.5 children. The feminine intuition which she usually ignored told her otherwise.

Granted that he was totally unsuitable, he was very attractive. She might even go so far as to admit that he was the most attractive man, married or otherwise, she had met. Barring her father. Given that there was always the chance that things would develop further, and that games of make-believe tended to lose their thrill and become plain exhausting, perhaps she should let on who she really was? But if things were fated not to develop, if he were due to run back to his wife in three weeks anyway, how foolish to miss out on so much fun simply because women with decent IQs affected his prowess. Perhaps his wife was a genius? Perhaps she never had time for him because she was too busy perfecting her cure for muscular dystrophy and knocking off a witty biography of Hegel? Perhaps she knew her?

Henry took another sip of her Martini. Oh God.

# Chapter Sixteen

Through his palm he could feel her heart slowing from a gallop to a canter. At her nearside temple a vein echoed the pulse. She was staring up at the metal beams, blinking away droplets of sweat as they were channelled into her eyes. An ambulance wailed below them, then away. The rain, torrential now, clattered on the roof. Sweat shone on her face, ran teasing down his spine to the hairs above his buttocks, formed a hybrid shadow on the sheet beneath them. She lay, stared, waited. He had to break the silence.

'I hurt you.'

'No.'

'I'm sorry.'

'Don't say that.'

'I'd say it's because I love you, but I don't know you at all so that would be a lie.'

'No. You don't.'

'Know you or love you?'

'Know me.'

Still she didn't move. She fired her short answers into the air over her head, like a child daring to let her spit fall back in her face. He had nearly not come.

After that absurd mistake over the telephone, his first impulse had been to go to take an extended refuge in bed. Hilary's voice had suggested her own so strongly that for a crucial moment he had forgotten that she didn't have his number. He could have asked Hilary round, but after claiming that a pupil called

Sandy was there it would have involved a heavy-handed lie. Hilary's importunate tone had maddened him. What had he said? Let's leave it for a bit? No. Far worse. Let's let it go. Just let it go. Back in his room he realized what he had done and found himself running back to the hall and dialling the number, but Hilary's line was engaged.

He returned to his flat, made himself a stiff gin and French and drifted from a stab at some Scriabin to some easier Prokofiev and thence to a new magazine. The adrenalin was searing through his system, however, and the alcohol only heightened its effects. Icy glass in hand, he hurried clumsily back to the hall and called the number a second time.

'Hil? Hi . . . Yes. Look, I'm sorry. It looks as though Sandy's going to leave early. Can you still come round? . . . Great! See you in about half an hour? . . . Great. 'Bye. And look . . . I'm sorry.'

There was nothing in the fridge but some sausages which had passed their sell-by date and a *piña colada*-flavoured yoghourt. Rufus snatched up the brown envelope that served as his wallet and slipped out to Marylebone High Street. The supermarket was still open. A musak version of one of the songs from Hilary's execrable musicals was being played. Rufus could never remember which was which. This was 'Going out to Surrey' or something equally unlikely. He scoured the shelves for something quick that still looked thought out and listened to the coconut clip-clop of the musak pony.

Midway between bananas and lavatorial blue-rinse he was held up by a voluminous Turkess with a trolley, stared at a packet of Coco Pops and realized how narrowly he had just avoided losing the most important person in his life. His eyes caught those of the baby on a disposable nappy pack and he knew that he loved Hilary, that the knowledge that he was even now risking life and limb on that dreadful old bicycle brought the sharpest joy, that if just now he had cut himself off from that daft good humour, that recuperative trust, that bottomless fund of sympathetic support, his life would be inexpressibly empty. He had put all this in jeopardy for a glorified masseuse who was . . . well, yes, who was admittedly extraordinary in bed and *was* possessed of a rare pair of arms, as well as a fast car and a steady income, but whom he didn't know at all. He knew nothing whatsoever about Sandy save, vaguely, how she earned her keep and how her deep voice sounded across a pillow in the dark. Of her personal life, of her needs and responsibilities, he was wholly ignorant. Quite possibly she would vanish back into a semi-marriage tomorrow and he would have lost all hope of keeping Hilary.

Suddenly impatient and beginning to sicken with fear, Rufus snatched up and paid for a bottle of overpriced claret, two helpings of Cordon Bleu Kitchen ready-made Chicken Kiev, and a tub of Hilary's preferred American pecan ice cream. There wasn't time for a bath, but he changed out of his suit into jeans and a clean shirt. He didn't shave; Hilary liked stubble.

The bell rang before he had time to do anything with food.

'Hi.'

'Hello,' said Hilary.

'Come on up.' He looked terrible. His eyes were dark-stained beneath, and still tear-puffed. His face was drawn, tension creased into his forehead. His tread on the stairs ahead of Rufus was heavy, hesitant. 'Sorry, I haven't had time to cook anything much, but . . .'

'Oh, you needn't do . . .'

'No, it won't take twenty minutes. All pre-done. Drink?'

'Thanks.' He wanted to hug him, but Hilary was all at the wrong angle somehow; all elbow and bicycle pump. Rufus made him a gin and tonic and refreshed his own gin and French. Hilary had sat in an armchair rather than on the sofa and had crossed his legs. 'Thanks,' he said to the gin, then, 'don't bother to cook, Roof.'

'Don't be silly. It's no trouble.' Hilary sighed and gulped some gin as Rufus pulled the packaging off the chicken. 'Look,' he went on, 'I'm really sorry about what I said earlier.'

'No. For God's sake, don't be. You were right.'

'What?' Oh Christ. He dumped the chicken. Hilary turned.

'You were right.' He was on the verge of tears, his voice harsh and uneven. 'We *should* "let it go".' Rufus could only stare. 'It's all wrong. I'm all wrong. We both want different things and neither of us is prepared to . . .'

'It's my fault,' Rufus interrupted. 'I don't think properly

before I . . .'

'No. Please, Rufus, just let me . . . I mean . . . Earlier tonight.
I knew you were right. It's just that you were braver than me
and faced up to it first.' Hilary stood. His voice was evening
out; he was in control. He might even be relieved to be saying
all this. 'Look,' he walked over and took Rufus' hands in his.
His fingers were frozen. Cue the Puccini. 'I need a spouse and
you . . . well, you need a lover.' He choked on his words and
Rufus felt his eyes prick and his throat tauten. Hilary fell
forward and hugged him hard, rubbing a hand on his back as
to a frightened child. 'It just won't work.' Rufus raised his
hands and crushed his arms against Hilary's back. 'It would be
unfair of me to make you even try and if we . . .' Here he
sniffed heavily, his voice almost deafening by Rufus' ear. 'If we
stop now, then at least we won't end up loathing each other.'

'I blew it,' Rufus managed to mumble. The verb seemed
fatuous of a sudden. Balloons. Feathers. Toy trumpets. Party
poopers. 'It's me. I blew it.'

'No.' Hilary pulled back and took Rufus' face in his hands.

'Christ, this is all so corny,' thought Rufus. 'If he says he
blew it too, I'll laugh.'

'We *both* blew it.' Rufus' snigger came out as a strangled
cough. 'It was heaven sometimes, but usually it was hell on
earth. You *know* that's true.'

By a supreme effort, Rufus forced himself not to cry. He
sought a role and found it by taking up his gin. The action of
swallowing the bitter iced liquid released the tension in his
throat. He sighed and walked past Hilary into the sitting
room. He picked up Hilary's bike pump where it lay by the
young man's barely touched gin and tonic. It was black with a
blue stripe; it said 'Kingfisher' on it, but the kingfisher transfer
had rubbed off, leaving only the bird's head and a snapped-off
beak.

'Can I see you again?' Rufus asked. A street-lamp was
falling sick, turning on for seven seconds and off for five, then
on for ten and off for three, then on for four and off again.

'Let's wait and see. I'm not sure it's a good idea. We
might . . .' Hilary's voice petered out. He walked up beside
him. 'We're both very weak. Let's just see.' Gently he took the
pump from Rufus' grasp. He touched his chilly fingers across

his stubbled cheek then laid a hand briefly on his shoulder, squeezed, and walked quietly from the flat.

Off for eight, then on for five and off for five. A faint drizzle was starting to fall. When the light was on it lit the haze of droplets. Down below, Hilary's padlock chain clanked as he slung it over one shoulder. His dynamo sighed into action as he rode off towards Baker Street. Rufus finished his drink, then picked up Hilary's glass and drained it in several gulps. He stood for a moment, two glasses in hand, and belched up the tonic bubbles. Absently he slipped the slice of lime into his mouth and chewed on it.

It would take all of forty minutes to reach Hammersmith. He had to set out at once. He threw the Chicken Kiev to join the neglected sausages in the fridge and, taking the ice cream in one hand and an overcoat in the other, he followed Hilary from the flat, telephoning Sandy from the pay-phone in the hall.

He had to change bus en route, getting soaked and steadily angrier as he stood in the penetrating drizzle on Notting Hill Gate. Had he made no second call to White City there would still have been tears, though Hilary usually drove his misery into housework or frenetic washing of hair. The engaged line had meant that he was calling queeny Richard or that drama cow Bridget, telling all. *South Pacific* or something suitably tasteless would have blasted out while Hilary bathed and pulled on tarty clothes; old jeans and a leather jacket. He would have got drunk with Bridget, picking lugubriously over a wasted eighteen months, then gone dancing with Richard to celebrate freedom regained. Rufus reflected with considerable bitterness that Hilary had dressed down in advance and was probably off to drink and dance in any case, which was why he couldn't stay to eat. For his part, he had been 'dancing' without Hilary for the past eighteen months, and always drank his gloom in solitude.

By the time Sandy's video entryphone was shining in his face, he had beaten himself into a fury. Her Martinis had gone unquaffed.

'It's my wife, you see,' he muttered, shamefaced. 'She's always domineering, always in control. I . . . I need an outlet.'

'Ssh. I don't need to know.'

'But I don't want you to think it's because I don't like you. It's because I . . . I could like you so much.'

At last she swung her head on the pillow and turned her gaze full upon him. One eye was in shadow, the other glistened.

'It's strange,' she murmured, 'but I find it sort of helps.'

'How?'

'Because of her — your wife. I know so little about her and you and . . . what you did just now helped me to feel I was yours.'

'You're mine,' he said. 'Please. You're mine.'

He slipped a hand over the deepening bruise on her neck and brushed her lips with his. It was a trick of the light, of course, but for a moment she reminded him curiously of Hilary.

# Chapter Seventeen

Fed and changed, Dan was sleeping once more in his cot. Hilary had woken from a night broken alternately by guilt and spasms of liberated joy to a morning of supportive blue clarity. Inspired by this reminder of what Spring would be like when it chose to arrive, he had donned his tracksuit and, feet under the armchair, was grunting through fifty sit-ups. Overheated, he was beginning to feel fairly sick around the mid-thirties, when Mrs Sharma called up from his hall. She was agitated. She rounded the stairs and met him on the landing.

'Your doorbell is broken, so I had to let him in,' she puffed.

'Who?' asked Hilary.

'He's come to take the baby. I know he has.'

At that moment the man came round the stairs behind her.

'Hello,' said Hilary. 'Sorry about the bell. Thanks, Mrs Sharma.'

She threw him a glance that bordered on the despairing, then shuffled downstairs.

'Mr Metcalfe?'

'That's right.'

'Neville Cutts, your area health visitor.'

'Hello,' said Hilary again, shaking hands and leading him into the living room. 'My sister sent you?'

'Your sister?' He was stocky, with short blond hair and scarcely any lip. A thick Norwegian jersey and leather bomber jacket accentuated the 'aggressive look'.

'Yes. Doctor Metcalfe up at Princess Marina's. She said she would send for someone.'

'Could be. I only received a memo. I gather we owe you an apology.'

'Oh, well. I'd hardly say . . .'

'It should have been a routine matter. Matron Parsons at the clinic misunderstood. Of course, if you'd like to make a note of any expenses, we'll refund what we can.' He glanced around the room at the nappies, the bucket, the cot, the anorak. 'You seem to have . . .'

'Oh no,' Hilary laughed. 'My landlady sent me all this. Except for the carrycot, of course. He came in that.'

'Came?'

'I mean that was how I found him. Under the flyover, in the carrycot.' Hilary remembered the drifting snow, the thin wail in the dark and his bitterness when Rufus was not on the train. Neville Cutts strode over to the cot. No briefcase. No identification. He might be anyone.

'Ah. Asian,' he said. 'They didn't tell me that. No illnesses of any kind?' He opened out the carrycot and was pulling back Dan's bedding.

'No. But there's no need now.' Hilary hurried over, irritated that Mrs Sharma had ever let the man in. 'You see, there's no need to take him away. I'm filing for an adoption.'

'Yes, well, that's why I'm here. We think we've found a suitable family. Of course he'll have to go to a home in the interim. Asian . . . they should have told me.'

'No, you don't understand. I mean that I'm going to adopt him myself. I'll keep him. You shouldn't have been called, really. Another misunderstanding. I'm sorry to have wasted your time.' It was only as he tried to shrug that Hilary felt how tense he was.

'Have you filled in an AD783?'

'No. I don't think so.'

'You have to do these things through the right channels.'

'Well, perhaps you'd be so kind as to have one sent to me.'

Neville Cutts turned and leaned on the end of the cot, an eyebrow raised. 'And how would you propose to support your child?'

'I work. I'm a teacher. I earn enough for two. Just about.'

'And during the day?'

'I rarely work a full day, and when I do Mrs Sharma from downstairs has offered to babysit.'

'Has she now?'

'Yes.'

'And what about that?' He pointed a hairy hand at the bedside table. In their Durham days, Bridget had smuggled him a copy of *The Joy of Gay Sex* from America. He had never been so unspontaneous as to consult the thing *in media res*, but it was a fascinating read on lonely nights. Now he wished he had got around to making a brown paper binding.

'Oh,' he said, 'that.'

'You're gay, I take it?'

Hilary snatched wildly at red herrings. My artistic cousin from Iowa City, Iowa? The previous tenant? Idle curiosity?

'Yes,' he confessed, 'but that's irrelevant at the moment because I'm single.'

'But how long for? According to our research, homosexuals are never single for as long as heterosexual men.'

'Aren't we lucky?' Hilary's blood was up and he could hear his voice rising in pitch. 'Maybe we're more lovable. Maybe we're just more honest with questionnaires.'

'Surely you don't think two blokes could bring up a kid properly? If they managed to stay together, that is.'

'Why ever not? Did your mother bring you up "properly"?'

'Well . . . I'

'You can't give an unequivocal yes?'

'But a baby needs a mother.'

'Like a monkey needs a pressure cooker.'

'It's only *natural*.'

'So are wasps, Mr Cutts, and bilharzia.'

'I don't need this, Mr Metcalfe. I don't have time or, to be quite frank, much interest.'

So saying, Neville Cutts plucked the protesting Daniel from his cot and swung him into the carrycot. That was too much.

'Don't you *dare* touch my baby!' Hilary heard himself spit. He snatched the carrycot and gave Cutts a shove towards the landing. He had forgotten his height. As the intruder beat a hasty retreat to the stairs, Hilary felt a surge of surprised triumph. Cutts all but shook a fist.

'You'll be hearing from us, Metcalfe,' he blurted, impotent. 'Your sort don't stand a chance.'

'Bye,' Hilary returned sweetly, hugging the bellowing carrycot to his chest and wondering if he were perhaps a little hysterical. Within minutes of the front door's slamming it reopened. There was a thunder of wellington boots on the stairs and Mrs Sharma, transformed by the scent of battle, was at his side.

'You keep him, then?' she asked, eyes bright. 'Will you keep the *charulata*?'

'I'll try, *Shrimati Sharma*,' he said, baby in his arms. 'With your help, I'll try.'


In recent years Hilary's godmother Evelyn had become a lonely do-gooder. With the speed of a Jacobean last act, her life had been stripped of its familiar trappings. There had been a scandal involving her husband's criminal insanity and eventual suicide (in police custody), which had won her sympathy but lost her several friends. Her daughter had finished at Cambridge and moved to America. Her son – a violinist whom Rufus had met once or twice and declared insufferable – lived off Ladbroke Grove with a curiously dull sculptor. Six years ago the school she ran for deaf children had been closed after the withdrawal of its local government grant. Evelyn had announced herself to be too old for a new post and had sold both school and house, retiring to a pretty cottage off the top of Hampstead High Street. She had bought a springer spaniel, called Bids, to replace the children in her life and, between strenuous walks on the Heath, devoted her free time to unpopular causes and the Citizens' Advice Bureau. She was a second cousin of Hilary's father. Since the latter's removal to Paris, she had taken her godmotherly duties seriously. She had met Rufus and, shared musical passions notwithstanding, had disapproved of him wholeheartedly. Evelyn knew all. Well, most.

Hilary's school duties finished at two today, and he spent the next hour crossing West London to Baker Street and riding thence, via Regent's Park, to Swiss Cottage and Haverstock Hill. Evelyn opened the front door while he was locking his bicycle to the railings; she and Bids greeted him warmly and led him through to the little sitting room at the rear. The back of the house, which looked on to a miniature garden, was masked by an old *magnolia grandiflora* which reached almost to the tiles. The wind caused its horny leaves to scratch on the windows like a storm-shocked cat.

Though little of her furniture had changed, the feeling of the place was in poignant contrast to the atmosphere of the old house in Keats Grove. Where she had once been active within an ordered space, now she seemed still amid clutter. The sitting room in particular had a strong grandmotherly flavour. She had bought him his favourite walnut cake, and had even made some sandwiches. As he sat on the sofa, he was moved to see that she now kept the kettle and tea-caddy beside her desk to save herself the walk to the kitchen. He asked for news of her children, Venetia and Seth, and smiled to hear her pride in their doings and her proud hiding of the fact that they neglected her. Finally, having poured them both tea, she sank into the sofa too and fixed him with her startling green stare.

'Tell me about this baby,' she demanded.

He told all; far more than he had told his sister. He told her of the carrycot in the subway, his rebuffal at the clinic, Mrs Sharma's unlooked-for kindness and Dan's many charms. Then he paused to call Bids in from chasing sparrows in the garden and to cut them both slices of cake. At her prompting he told her of Henry's possible envy, of Neville Cutt's wounding insinuations, and of his own desire – which had hit him with the force of an epiphany – to become the boy's adoptive parent. Evelyn poured herself another cup of tea, pushed Bids off her lap and walked to the window. The chilly sunlight caught the silver bun of her hair.

'You're not really happy as a teacher, are you, Hil?' It was more statement than inquiry.

'No,' he agreed. 'I think I'm enjoying it more than I did, though. I expect less, so I tend to get pleasantly surprised.'

'How about acting?'

'Well,' he faltered. She was playing her old game of cutting straight to the heart of his pain. He complied; one couldn't lie to those eyes. 'There's not really enough time. It's embarrassing getting time off for auditions, and I'm too exhausted for many dance classes – for any, in fact.'

'You've lost your sense of vocation?'

'Yup. I still practise now and then, and sure, if a man wound down his window and said, "Hey kid, you wanna be in

95

movies?" I'd come running, but . . .'

'But you've . . .?'

'Yup.'

He took another slice of cake and felt miserable.

'How's Rufus?'

'Fine. I think. Still teaching. I was going to see him last night but . . . well . . . with Dan and everything.' He experienced anew a dizzying sense of his new liberty and a twinge of the pain it was causing him. Now was not the time to tell her.

'Hilary, children make hopeless cement. If things are going to fall apart, they will; babies are just one more thing to hold above the wreckage. You've just admitted to hating your job, having no future and a lousy love life. Why in God's name do you want a baby?'

'I feel sorry for him.'

'He won't thank you for that.'

'Yes, but other people's problems . . .'

'Make one's own seem small. I know, but once you adopt him he won't have any problems and you'll just have another one, big and growing.' She smiled at his gloomy face and came to sit beside him again, resting a firm hand on his arm. 'I'm being vile. It's only because you've got no real mother. I don't count dear Marie-Claude, and Henrietta has so obviously got something else on her mind. I'm just trying to make you decide what you think. Do you *truly* care what happens to Dan?'

'Yes.'

'More than teaching?'

'Certainly.'

'What do you earn?' He told her. She hid her shock well. 'Could you live on half that, if your rent were paid?' she asked.

'Just about,' he said after a moment's thought.

'Then hand in your notice and go on the dole at the end of term. You've only another term to teach this year anyway, isn't that so?'

'Yes. If the woman I replaced is coming back.'

'Get Mrs Chammy-thingy to look after him during the day for the last few weeks. Explain when you sign on why you had to leave work. They'll give you just about enough a week to live on, plus something for Dan – milk and so on – plus your rent. If you really can't manage, then bloody well ask your father. He's not as square as he was – Marie-Claude has seen to that – he's rich as Croesus and you'll have given him a grandchild. After the first year, you'll be free to start going to auditions again. And if the whole thing's absolutely dire and you decide that children are an abomination after all, you can get the poor thing adopted again.'

'But how do I adopt him in the first place?' asked Hilary, excited.

'Oh, that's the simplest part. In a couple of days that little man will get a summons sent to you, demanding your appearance before a DHSS tribunal. Go, explain that you're adopting Dan. They'll try to dissuade you with phoney arguments about stability, emotional security, rates and so forth. Ignore them. Just tell them you're being represented by Dr Hannah Flowers, whose card you'll find in that box on my desk. No the red one. That's it. Tell them that, read anything they ask you to sign, then leave. You don't have to sign anything immediately – you can even ask for a day to think it over or consult your lawyer. Hannah will do the rest.'

'Who is she?'

'An old friend of my poor Huw's from Cambridge. Batty American lawyer moved to London. She specializes in custody and adoption; especially gay cases.' Hilary felt himself redden. 'She's just finished winning a child from the husband of a friend of mine.'

'Who for?'

'My friend and her friend, Emma.'

'Ah.' Hilary bent Hannah Flowers' card between his fingers. 'Won't she be terribly expensive?' he asked.

'Not really. Anyway, she'll send the bills to me.'

'But . . .'

'Happy birthday, darling.'

'You can't possibly.'

'Of course I can. I'm rolling nowadays. Well, relatively rolling. More rolling than you'll ever be.'

Hilary laughed and hugged her. She held him tighter than he had expected. He wondered when the insufferable Seth had last paid her a visit. She suggested a walk on the Heath. He offered to walk her a part of the way, but reminded her that he had to be back to say good night to Dan.

'Of course. You're on your bicycle.'

'Yes. Why?'

'I'd forgotten. You'd better go now. I won't go for a walk. Bids has been once already today and it's turning rather cold again.'

'Oh, but it would be fun.'

'No. And you must get back before it gets dark. The roads are so dangerous now.'

He felt he had spoilt something. The least he could have done was to walk with her. He knew from experience however that, once decided, she was immovable. She stood in the doorway as he walked back to his bike.

'Evelyn.'

'Yes?'

'How much do you know about adoption? Is there a chance I won't get him?'

'Very little. It would be different if he were from a home or had parents or, let's be frank, were white, but abandoned babies are much simpler; fewer strings attached. There'll be legal forms to sign, and a hearing. I'll see Hannah about it tomorrow. She'll get in touch after you've given her name to the tribunal thingy.'

'Right.' Seeing her gaunt frame leaning on the doorpost, hands rubbing against the cold, he wanted to make amends and say thank you. He had an idea. 'What are you doing tonight, about eight-thirty?' he called out, swinging a leg over his saddle.

'Nothing. Why?'

'Come round. I'm going to organize a sort of christening supper. Please come.'

'Yes, please. I'll find something special in the cellar.'

He launched off down Haverstock Hill again. Poor thing, he thought. He lived so far away, yet she had accepted with alacrity.

# Chapter Eighteen

Sumitra sat on her bunk bed over the freezers, swinging her legs and holding a book.

'Unsex me here,' she said, staring absently at her pillow, 'and fill me . . . fill me.' She glanced at her book, then looked back at the pillow with a frown of private impatience, continuing with a metrical nodding of the head, 'Yet I do fear thy nature it is too full of the milk of human kindness to catch the nearest way thou wouldst be great art not without ambition . . .'

She knew that her bedroom was different from those of other children. No one else she knew slept with a brace of chest freezers for company. No one else she knew was a handmaid of the Prince Goddess; it was meet and right that her bedroom should be strange, for so was the truth to which she bore witness. All the same, Sumitra was grateful that her parents did not encourage her to bring home friends. The only children to visit her were those of their own acquaintance, and they had not penetrated beyond the airless formality of the sitting room with its religious statuettes and gaudy calendar. She disliked these children for their shyness and stupidity, and would scare them by speaking only English. If pressed, she would take them out to the yard to play *ikki dukki*, but never would she take them to her room.

At a birthday party she had once seen a white girl's bedroom and been scandalized at its bridal luxury. Her own was set out from the main body of the terrace, at the end of an extension which housed the main bathroom and garage. It would have been the garage, in fact, but they had no car. Her mother had taped up the sliding door to keep out draughts, and had a bunk bed fixed on one wall. It was an eccentric arrangement with which the girl had grown up. She cherished it. She was proud of the ladder she climbed to bed, and of the smart linoleum patterned like green crystals. She had a stretch of rug between her bunk and the door so that she could walk barefoot to the bathroom without chilling her feet. Three pictures were pinned above her bed. One was a little poster of Amabaji, the divine mother, who seemed so sad now that the *Narendra* had proved her redundant. The others were old black and white photographs of the house in Surat where her father had grown up, and of he and *Ba* with *Dadaji* and *Ma* on their wedding day, solemn in the sun. *Ma* had been forever telling her about the Indian sun, and the smells and the flowers, but Sumitra had smiled as she had smiled at her grandmother's funny tales of the elephant god and the monkey general, without belief. Born in Hammersmith, she knew nothing of Greenwich, let alone India. The sea, too, she had dismissed as a myth, until she saw it on a television in a shop window and asked *Ba* what it was. She had a white wardrobe for her clothes and a wooden chair where *Ma*, her grandmother, used to sit to tell her stories of Ganesh and Hanuman. *Ma* was dead now, and the *Narendra* gave her *Shri Shakespeare*'s strange play to read instead.

In the main body of the house her father swore suddenly, and a plate smashed on the kitchen floor. Sumitra stopped her recitation and listened. He had shouted little since the days before her sister, Kamala, left. Tonight he raved because he had guessed that *Ba* had been to see her in secret. *Ba* was hopeless at lying, and so *Baba* was smashing a plate.

Kamala was eight years Sumitra's senior. She had rebelled and was officially dead. First she had refused to wear Hindu clothes, changing from her school uniform into a pair of borrowed jeans or a mini-skirt. Then she had rubbed off her *tilah*, and taken to wearing eyeshadow and splashes from a bottle of scent called *Charlie*. She had cut off her glossy plait so that her hair was like a boy's. Every night there had been appalling arguments as she hurried through her homework, then got dressed to go out with white friends from school. *Baba* would shout and say she was no daughter of his, *Ma* had cried that her grandchild was a disgrace, *Ba* had wept in a corner and Kamala had shouted louder than any of them, calling *Baba* an old fool and a tyrant. When she left school she had ignored *Baba*'s arrangement for her to marry Prakash, the handsome boy whose father owned the electrical shop in Wood Lane, and she had taken a job as a sales assistant in Oxford Street. Sumitra had only been there once, when her mother had wanted to buy more of the thermal underwear she wore beneath her *saris*. It was at the time when the English celebrated their dying god's first birth and the trees had been full of lights and delicious hot air had blown from the top of the shop doors. It was unutterably lovely, and she could not see why her father pretended that it was such an evil place where Kamala would meet her ruin. For a while Kamala had lived beside them in the house, coming home only to sleep and eat, barely acknowledged by *Baba*, then Prakash's father had come round in a rage and said that a wealthy white man dropped her off every evening and kissed her in public as if she were a whore. There was a final battle, which ended in Kamala admitting that the man was the owner of her shop and that she was pregnant by him. She was thrown out the same night, and the family had to go into mourning. This had not been difficult for Sumitra, since she had worshipped her sister and missed her sorely.

That had been months ago and Sumitra hadn't seen her sister since. She suspected that her mother paid her secret visits, but was only told so tonight. *Ba* had slipped into her room half an hour ago, looking frightened, rain on her hair. Kamala was well, she said, and living in a flat in Brook Green. She had sent her little sister a perfect white cardigan from the shop. It had tiny buttons of plastic ivory. *Baba* was not to be told. She was to tell him that the garment was a present from her Aunt Lakshmi in Southall.

As she listened to her voice rising against his once more, Sumitra was happy that her mother had been on secret missions. The woman's tearful compliance with *Baba*'s severity had made her fear lest she took his old-fashioned ideas seriously. What he called Kamala's 'sin' was perfectly understandable. White men like *Shri Metcalfe* were far more beautiful than *Baba*'s dreadful friends and cousins in their ugly anoraks and flared trousers. Western women, like Lady Macbeth and the women teachers at school, were overblown and awkward however, and she saw no point in mimicking their style of dress. Her mother's thermal underwear solution was the best, although the Wellington boots spoiled the effect.

There were steps in the corridor and her parents came in. They had macs on and *Ba* was tying a headscarf.

'Darling,' she said, 'your *Baba* and I are off to the Centre to see a film. Can we trust you to go to bed on your own?'

'Of course,' said Sumitra, hiding *Macbeth* since they wouldn't approve of the cover, let alone the subject matter.

'Within the hour?'

'Yes, *Baba*.'

'Nightie-night, then.'

' 'Night.'

She leaned forward on her bunk and kissed her mother, then presented her forehead for her father's kiss.

'We'll lock the front door after us,' he said. 'Sleep well.'

She could hardly believe her luck. She waited until she heard the front door close, then scurried down her ladder. She peered out of the window, through the pouring rain to the *Narendra*'s flat. All the lights were on and she could hear the usual music. He was celebrating. She would celebrate too. Standing on tip-toe, she thrust a hand beneath her mattress and pulled out a thick brown envelope, then hurried to the living room. Without turning the light on, she lifted back the curtain and looked along the street. *Ba* and *Baba* were waiting at the stop for the Gujurati Centre. As she watched, they boarded a bus. She let the curtain fall and switched on the standard lamp.

There was an old gramophone behind the sofa. *Ma* had liked to play records of religious songs and of music from Indian musicals to remind her of the sun and the flowers. Sumitra tugged it out and plugged in its flex. It was a second-hand model and took some time to warm up. Eyes alight, she reached into the envelope and pulled out the possession she prized next only to the photograph from the Starbright Agency. It was evil of her, really; even handmaids to the World were not meant to steal. The spare key to *Shri Metcalfe*'s flat, which dangled on a hook in the kitchen, had proved too much temptation though, and last week she had crept up there when she knew he was out. It was so small, she was sure he would not miss it quickly, and she promised herself she would replace it before the month was done. For the first time that day she stared at the little record's cover. She had to read the words before she played the mystic song.

' "Capital Stereo Record",' she mouthed. ' "The Full Spectrum of Sound. From the soundtrack of the motion picture Rodgers and Hammerstein's *The King and I*, a Twentieth Century-Fox Cinemascope-55 Picture." '

Breathless, she flicked the old brown lever and watched the tone-arm jerk out over the forty-five. She sat back and stared at every lovely detail of the cover picture as the strings played the four-bar oom-cha oom-cha introduction.

A woman sat on a footstool. She had bright ginger hair, scarlet lips and the biggest dress Sumitra had ever seen, off the shoulders and spread out like a cinema curtain down below, in violet silk. A handsome bald man, with Asiatic features, in equally splendid clothes (though in brown and gold to match the footstool), stood with one foot on the stool beside her and his forefinger pointing curiously at the ceiling. She was looking down in modesty. Sumitra had decided that he was proposing they go upstairs to make a baby at once. The woman's voice was high and extremely English, like a newscaster.

'It's a very ancient saying, but a true and honest thought,' she enunciated over the music, 'that if you become a teacher, by your pupils you'll be taught.' Here she launched into the loveliest singing voice Sumitra had ever heard. She was undoubtedly *Shri Metcalfe*'s heavenly mother. 'As a teacher I've been learning, you'll forgive me if I boast, that I've now become an expert in the subject I love most; getting to know you.'

'Aah!' laughed the Siamese princesses.

# Chapter Nineteen

The afternoon's downpour had been such that the car park under her building was awash. Stepping out of her car, Henry had found it deeper than she had imagined. She had pegged up her tights over the bath and was stuffing her shoes with newspaper when the telephone rang. It was Marie-Claude.

' 'Allo, darling.'

'M–C, how are you?' she laughed, falling back on to the chaise-longue.

'I 'ave the most terrible cold, but I feel all the better for 'earing you.'

'Oh. Poor thing. I've got so much *news* though!'

'*Dis-moi, alors.*'

'You'll never believe it.'

'Try me.'

'I've got a man.'

There was a satisfying pause, then Marie-Claude asked cautiously. 'Is 'e there now?'

'Course not.'

There was a delighted whoop from the other end. 'But *minou*, that's such fun! What's 'e like?'

Smiling despite herself, Henry swung her bare legs up so that she could lie down. 'Well,' she began, 'he's tall – about six two – and broad-chested, and he's got dark brown hair and a marvellous, rather sly face, and he's younger than me, probably a commando in secret and he's called Andrew. Oh, and he's married, too.'

'My *dear*! Isn't that . . . er . . . Can you cope?'

'M–C, it's wonderful. I feel younger than I've . . .' She was

interrupted by the door buzzer. 'Oh Christ, M–C, that's him now and I haven't heard any of your news. I'll try and ring you later, OK?'

'OK, my dear,' her stepmother laughed. '*Ciao.*'

' 'Bye.'

She skipped to the intercom and looked at him on the video screen. He was carrying something. He was drenched. She could eat him.

'Come on up,' she said and pressed the lock control. She went to her wardrobe, unzipping her work skirt, and tugged on an old pair of jeans. Suddenly there was a high-pitched bleeping from her briefcase. She swore and limped back to the telephone. The jeans were on the tight side.

'Hello. Dr Metcalfe. You paged me.'

'Oh, great,' chirped the answering service girl. 'We've had a call from the police. Residential complaints on the Grosvenor Estate, Lillie Road. Apparently it's one of yours. Nancy Phelps. She's making too much noise and the police suspect she's anti-socially deranged. Can you go?'

'Damn.'

'Sorry?'

She heard Andrew open and shut the door. He put his hands around her waist and ground himself affectionately against her rear. She reached an absent-minded hand onto his thigh as she talked.

'I said "Damn". It's not terribly convenient.'

'You're the only person on, I'm afraid.'

'But what about Helen and Jock?'

He walked into the bathroom and shut the door.

'Sorry?'

'What about Dr Stevens or Dr Jonas?'

'She's having to work late and Jock's off with 'flu.'

'OK,' she sighed. 'What's the address?'

'Flat 47,' whined the girl, 'Walpole Tower, Vanbrugh Drive. Have you got an *A to Z*?'

'Yes, thanks,' Henry snapped. 'Tell them I'll be there in ten minutes, would you?' Perhaps this would be a good time to explain what she really did. Perhaps not.

'Right you are, then. Police Constable Rivers will be waiting by in case there's any difficulty. We'll send a van down, too.'

'Great,' she said, dead-pan.

'You're welcome.'

She turned to face Andrew as he emerged from the bathroom. The lavatory was flushing.

'Hi,' she said, 'you're soaked.'

'I know,' said he and pulled her towards him. They kissed. He pulled back for a moment, his eyes searching her face.

'Again,' she said, and they kissed again. There was something musky splashed on his jaws. It was bitter on her tongue. 'I stink,' she said, 'I haven't had a bath yet.'

'Well, you have a bath,' he said, and pecked her forehead, 'and when you return I shall have made,' he produced a carrier bag from behind his back, 'supper!' he exclaimed, and imitated a fanfare.

Her face fell. 'Oh shit, I'm sorry,' she said.

So did his. 'Why?'

'I've got to go out for a bit. That was work on the 'phone.'

'Work?' he demanded.

This was definitely not the moment to tell him what she really did.

'Yes. There's a bit of an emergency, you see. A man put his back out and I'm the only one on call tonight. It's very near here, in fact. I'll be back within the hour.'

'I thought you only worked during the day, visiting hospitals.'

'Well, I do, but sometimes I have to work at nights too, for overtime.' She started to look for her coat and some dry shoes. She hated PC Rivers, but at the same time she suspected that Andrew was about to prove extremely childish and was prepared to hate him too. 'Now I must rush. Make yourself at home. There are candles in the drawer of the table if the lights go out. The telly's on the blink, but the radio works . . . sort of. It is sweet of you to buy supper. I'll be back by nine at the latest.' No, Henrietta, that's quite wrong. 'But look . . .' she blurted on. 'Don't bother to make it unless you really want to.'

'Don't worry,' he said, dumping the bag on the floor. 'I won't.'

He turned on his heel and stalked out, leaving the door ajar. She stood listening to him stepping into the lift.

'Andrew?' she said, then louder, 'Andrew? Wait a bit.'

The lift door closed as she hurried on to the landing. The lights over the door were clicking on and off. Three. Two. If she raced down the stairs and risked breaking her neck, she might just catch him. One. G. But there again, he had been absurd. She walked round the flat switching off lights. It wasn't her fault if PC Rivers thought someone was anti-socially deranged. Andrew hadn't even waited for an explanation; she hadn't asked him to buy supper. She locked the flat door. It was sweet of him, though. She summoned the lift. G. One. Two. Darkness pounced. The lift halted in the shaft with a moan and a belch. Henry began to grope her way down the stairs. She would have to call Paris on her return.

It was no surprise to find that the Grosvenor Estate had no emergency generator. It was solely by the light of her head-lamps that Henry found her way along Vanbrugh Drive and made out the tin title of Walpole Tower in the near-blinding rain. There was precious little sign of Constable Rivers. Precious little sign of anyone.

Henry turned up the collar of her mackintosh, pulled out her torch and scurried on to the porch. The wind was rising, whipping the water against the sides of the building. She leaned against the heavy swing doors and found herself in the stairwell. For a tower block with forty flats, there was an eerie lack of the common signs of life. No children raced on the stairs. No youths fooled with the lift. No women ran outside to save their soaking washing. No one welcomed anybody home or called anyone in to supper. Thin brushes were taped to the edges of the doors to keep out the draught, but the wind still came through, catching on them as it did so to produce a thin, chill sound like a rough cloth against glass.

'Constable Rivers?' she called, tentatively. There was no reply. She shone her torch around the walls and found a plan of the tower's residents. The ink had run in places, but she discerned that Flat 47 on the topmost floor was indeed inhabited by N. Phelps. In the car on the way over, Henry had racked her professional memories and her files for a trace of N. Phelps and had come up with a woman who had passed through Jock Jonas' care over a year ago. Nancy had run away during treatment, but had been tracked down by a social worker who had said that she was now quite well and living on a council estate.

107

Henry sighed and pushed through the next set of doors to find the lift. Gambling, she pressed the call button. The doors swung open, evincing the presence of at least a small emergency generator. The stench ground in her nostrils. She started forward, prepared to bear it for a few seconds, then stopped as her torch caught the face of quite the least washed old man she had seen in months. He seemed to be lying on the lift floor. He grinned up at her.

'Just in time, sweetheart,' he chuckled.

Hastily she reached over his head and pressed a button at random. The doors closed. Angry now, she took a deep breath and shouted,

'Constable Rivers? It's Dr Metcalfe.' There was no reply. 'I'm down here,' she added, then wished she hadn't.

'He's gone,' said a woman's voice behind her.

Henry spun round. The woman was holding open a door to flat number one. Her candle lit her from beneath; a scrawny neck, white of twisting eye and a melodramatic halo of tallow-grey hair.

'Oh, no. Has he?' asked Henry.

'He's gone,' the weird sister repeated. 'He waited but now he's gone. Friend of yours, was he?'

'No, not in the slightest. I mean, not at all.' The woman made as if to shut her door once more but Henry forestalled her. 'I'm the doctor he sent for. I gather there's some problem. Nancy Phelps, I think; on the top floor.'

'Yeah.' The woman froze. She spoke without turning back, just froze in her tracks. 'Been screaming the place down, she has.'

'I can't hear anything.'

'You will if you wait.'

'But surely,' Henry protested, 'the top floor . . . I mean, isn't that too far for the sound to. . .?'

'Listen.' The weird sister held an encrusted digit to her ear and Henry listened. There was a bloodcurdling scream from on high, distorted by its passage down the stairs. 'Told you,' laughed the woman, with no apparent concern and shut the door.

Henry ran out to the car to find her bag. A sedative would almost certainly be needed. On her way in, a shower of large pieces of glass smashed onto the pavement to her left. No body landed with them, but a small stool splintered on the tarmac a few feet away. Rivers had been and gone. The van, if it were coming, had yet to arrive. This was a job for Dr Metcalfe. *Toute seule.* Oh God!

While her figure was athletic, Henry's heart was not. Once she reached the penultimate floor, she had to sit on the stairs to regain her breath. The screaming had petered out when she was passing the eighth floor. Sitting in the darkness, she could hear that, though considerably quieter than before, all was not peaceful on the floor above. Furniture was being moved; less dragged from place to place than bumped on the floor in irregular tattoos. Occasionally something would smash to the ground – a bottle, or a glass. After each outburst, Nancy Phelps, if indeed it had been her who had screamed, could be heard sobbing. There was no other voice, but from this close it sounded as though she were being attacked. 'Anti-socially deranged' my foot, thought Henry. While the elusive PC Rivers was listening to neighbourly slander and dialling the funny farm, the poor woman was probably being raped by some local lout. Repeatedly.

Henry jumped up, bracing herself, and started up the stairs again. A notice was slung on a chain across the way to the top floor: 'Construction Unsafe' it read. 'No Residents Beyond This Point'. She paused, shining the torch around the stairs ahead. There were pools of water, certainly, but no gaping ravines or treacherous holes in view. The lift was all too occupied.

Suddenly the screeching started afresh.

'Coward,' jeered Henry at herself and clambered over the chain. This lack of curiosity among neighbours was unnatural. With neither light nor television, perhaps they were all in bed? The doors to Flats 45 and 46 stood ajar. She shone her torch into each and found them empty, it not quite derelict. Henrietta had never been timid, but the possibility that she might have just climbed in pitch darkness through a deserted tower block was more upsetting than she cared to admit.

'No!' screamed Nancy Phelps. 'No! Please, no! I couldn't help it. You seen I couldn't. I had to. I had to. Oh no!'

Her yells subsided as what sounded like an armchair was

tossed across the flat. Henry felt the vibration through her feet.

'Nancy! Nancy! I've come to help you. Open up,' she shouted and smote the door with her fist. It flew open. There was a flurry of wet wind, then silence. She stepped across the threshold.

Where the window had been smashed was an irregular star of rain. A curtain, half torn down, flapped like a broken bird.

'Nancy, where are you?'

Someone was weeping nearby. Henry shone her torch around the room. Paper was hanging down in strips from the walls. Polystyrene tiles chequered the floor, along with chunks of plasterboard. Somewhere water was dripping into a bucket. Not a stick of furniture was unmolested; chairs lay on their sides, cushions were gutted. The contents of the kitchen drawers were scattered everywhere, sharp instruments having been rammed into any available soft surface. A table was flickering gently and Henry beat the flames down with a cushion. The smell of burnt feathers brought a taste of panic to her senses. She followed the weeping with her torch. A small woman lay naked on the bed, her head and shoulders covered with one of the curtains. Sobs shook her. The sofa had been jammed across the bedroom doorway. Henry climbed across it and approached the bed.

'Nancy?' The sobs stopped. 'Nancy, who did this? Have they gone?'

Nancy said nothing, but flung herself into Henry's arms. Her flesh was clammy and cold. Henry sat on the edge of the bed, which smelt sharply of fresh urine.

'I couldn't stand any more,' Nancy sobbed. 'I told her I had to do it.' She started to pant.

'I can't bear it if she screams again,' thought Henry and reached for her bag. 'This will help her go away,' she soothed, and injected a strong sedative. Nancy flinched, then sank her head into Henry's lap. Down below an approaching bell jangled. The van.

'Now, tell me who did this?'

'My sister.'

'Where is she now, then?'

'Dead. She died last year.'

'But who did this just now?'

110

'She was angry, you see. 'Cause of what I done.'

'What was that?'

Nancy sighed, almost contentedly, as the drug coursed through her system.

'Because I ate her. I know it's terrible and I shouldn't have done it, but like I said, I couldn't help it. Not really.'

High up in the night, amid this whistling mayhem, the confession sounded almost plausible. Henry shivered . . . from the cold.

'Come on,' she said. 'We'll find you something to wear and take you away from her for a bit, till she calms down. Would you like that?'

'Yes, please. There's a dress over there. On the door.'

Henry lifted Nancy's head back on to the bed and walked to the door. By the light of the torch she found a summer frock; a neatly ironed floral print strangely unmolested in the chaos. She brought it back to the bed.

'Arms up,' she commanded and started to slip it over her charge's head. It would take some time to manoeuvre the stairs with one so sleepy, but with luck the ambulance men would meet them half-way. She longed for the sane rituals of the 'Nine O'Clock News'. There were those Martinis left in Sandy's fridge . . .

'She came back, you see,' confided Nancy, taking Henry's hand after they had pushed the sofa out of the way. 'Came back and said she'd do me over for what I done to her.' They were starting down the stairs when a plate smashed on the wall behind them. 'Ate her, I did, 'cause I was that jealous,' said Nancy and sneezed like a cat.

# Chapter Twenty

The conductor brought the bus ride to an abrupt end in Shepherd's Bush Road; arbitrary spite, it seemed, was reason enough. Somebody had gone to considerable trouble to remove the bus shelter roof and break it into small pieces on the pavement. As he stood, clothes blackening beneath the rain, icy-damp soaking through the soles of his shoes, Rufus' pocketed hands discovered that he had used up his final pound coin and had left his wallet in the grocery bag in Sandy's flat. Wet beyond care, he blew his nose richly into a rain-sodden handkerchief and struck out along the route to White City.

The herdsmen had long departed Shepherd's Bush. Wood Lane boasted three sickly trees. The motor sounds of heavy traffic were dulled behind the continuous agitation of water by wheel, like the unfurling of a limitless box of cooking foil or the drawing of a shower curtain without end.

She was no more a physiotherapist than he was Flash Gordon. He had been duped. She had played a role to mock his fantasies in the realization. Had he told the truth and shamed the devil, had he sat in her little sports car and said, 'I'm a bisexual concert pianist who gives piano lessons (and occasionally other services) while waiting for his first concert booking, and who now has the compulsion to neglect his boyfriend and pursue the bubble normality by going to bed with you,' she would still have lied. It seemed more likely than ever that she enjoyed a temporarily absent lover; this would explain why she didn't mind his being 'married'. He had betrayed Hilary so that she could play games. And now Hilary . . .

Rufus was forced off the pavement by a squadron of television executives with designer umbrellas. A passing taxi sent a small wave over his shoes and socks.

There was still time. He would trudge to North Pole Road. He would plead stress, plead love's confusion, beg time. Rain-soaked prodigals were so appealing. A pure and contrite heart thou wilt not despise, Hilary, especially a drenched one with a rueful smile and no change for a home-bound bus. He would halt. He would stammer. He would make as if to turn and go. Lured by his bluff disarray, Hilary would catch him by the sleeve and tug him inside. A toad-in-the-hole would be raising a golden crust in the oven and a chorus from *Carousel* would be jangling on the air. A pile of marking would wait half-done in a pool of light on the desk.

'You can stay, can't you, Roof?' Hilary would falter. 'I mean . . . after all I've said, it's entirely up to you.'

Contrition, the name is R. Barbour.

He reached the flyover and turned off into the subway. Suddenly into the well-lit dry, he was aware of his sopping condition. Water was actually squelching between his toes as he walked. A baby was crying up ahead. He rounded the bend into the main corridor beneath the road and made out an oblong form at the far end. As he drew closer he perceived a dark blue carrycot. The abandoned cries were issuing from the same. For all his dislike of things nursery, he was shocked at the brutality that could abandon a baby in such a place and on such a night. He clean forgot his own plight and hastened, curious, forward.

It passed dimly through his mind that a drama of unwanted baby might deflect any wrath with which Hilary might conceivably welcome him. He bent over to peer inside.

'Gotcha, wally!'

He had barely glimpsed the cassette recorder tucked under the blanket when strong hands seized his arms and pushed him roughly against the wall, face to the tiles. He made no attempt at self-defence beyond a brief struggle that was savagely quashed by a further shove against the wall. All the voices he heard, as hands dived into his pockets and frisked over his arms and legs, were female.

'What's 'e got, then?'

'Nuffink.'

'Bastard!'

Something struck him on the head. The blow hurt intensely and provided as good a reason as any for sinking, eyes closed, to the floor. There was a tough-booted kick to his left thigh, at which he almost cried out, and a gratuitous swivel of heel on hand which caused him to bite his tongue; then the 'baby' was silenced with a click and stout-booted footsteps receded.

Brief suicidal declines notwithstanding, Rufus had never found it easy to weep. As he sat up slowly against the wall, rubbing the burgeoning egg beneath his hair with one hand and sucking the bruised fingers of the other, there was a prickling in his eyes and a keen sense of personal injustice in his heart, but no tear stained his cheek. He rose, uncertainly. There was a stab of pain where his thigh had been kicked. Swearing, he limped out into the rain once more, torn between gratitude that his attackers had not held razors, shame at his cowardice at not putting up a fight, and loathing of babies in general and the paternal instinct in particular.

A pure, well, contrite-ish heart thou wilt not despise, Hilary, especially when it could pass muster as a drowned rat and has just been mugged by three – or shall we say five – lesbian gypsies.

A few yards into North Pole Road, a small boy was standing on the roof of a faintly familiar, elderly Volvo estate, throwing his entire weight into twisting off one of the windscreen wipers. Rufus saw a window sticker advertising a Cornish music festival and recognized the car as Evelyn Peake's, but was too tired to do anything but stare at the boy who, pausing in his vandalism, stared back.

Far from there being no light but the bachelor glow of a desk lamp, the windows of the flat were ablaze. Frowning as he drew near, Rufus could make out several voices singing drunkenly along with Shirley Bassey's rendition of the Bach/Gounod 'Ave Maria'. The curtains were all drawn, but there was a six-inch gap between two of them. He crossed to the other side of the street and shifted into the best view. His heart sank, his thigh throbbed and he began to feel extremely wet indeed as he saw first Evelyn, then Bridget, then Richard – laughing, in party hats. There were other guests he failed to recognize.

Hilary, who never threw parties, was finally throwing this one to celebrate their divorce.

A different window was thrown up. 'Rufus! Hi! Wait a second, I'm coming right down.'

It was Hilary. He had been watching him stare. Before Rufus could answer, the window was flung down once more and the sweet familiar face was gone. Rufus promptly lost what little nerve was left him. The thought of being hauled into the role of 'Little Matchgirl', of being kindly led, lame and dripping, amidst those sly laughs and knowing looks – possibly too, the thought that so public a reunion would be a little too final – sent him hobbling wildly into the night.

# Chapter Twenty-One

Bridget stood swaying against the table. She raised her glass in one hand and adjusted her pink party hat with the other. Her hair sprouted in auburn cascades; she had grown it to play Marianne in last year's BBC adaptation of *Sense and Sensibility* and had retained the look to play Perdita at the Old Vic. Hilary thought her Perdita execrable, but she had looked so appealing that no one else seemed to have minded much.

'I want to propose a toast,' she said, smiling round the table, 'to the latest addition to the one-parent-family statistics. Ladies and gentlemen, I give you Hilary and Daniel Metcalfe!'

'Daniel *Vaisey* Metcalfe,' corrected Evelyn, who had driven down with a case of port for when he grew up.

'Sorry,' Bridget continued, 'Daniel *Vaisey* Metcalfe.'

'Why Vaisey?' somebody asked.

'Old family name,' said Richard.

'All the men are lumbered with it,' added Hilary, 'and I thought it would appease Dad if I did the thing properly.'

It was so touching. Everyone Hilary had rung on returning from Hampstead had dropped whatever they were doing and said they could come. This solidarity in the face of his decision to adopt Daniel had brought home to him the enormity of his new undertaking. Certainly a few of them – Rich for instance, and Poppy – were supporting his action as that of a fashionable freak. They thought it 'perfectly marvellous' for a single person to adopt a baby, but had no intention of doing so themselves. Evelyn and, surprisingly, Bridget were more earnest in their support. Bridget had come early, as she had been rehearsing at the television centre, and had watched him make a lasagne and chop-up salad. She had enthused about Dan's prettiness, of course, but then her voice had filled with uncharacteristic gravity.

'You do realise, don't you Hil,' she said, 'that you may have to pretend to be straight?'

'Surely not?'

'Oh, yes. For men *and* for women now, they're very hot on so-called domestic morality. That means that if you don't have a live-in lover of three years' standing at the time of adoption, they'd prefer you to stay single rather than risk a parade of one-night-stands through the nursery.'


Now that the lasagne tin lay scraped bare before him, and Dan was asleep in the bathroom, he watched these good friends raise their glasses and felt almost weepy. To break up the sentiment, he jumped to his feet.

'Party time!' he declared and set a Julie Andrews record playing to unanimous groans of delight. As he put the plates to soak in the kitchen and went about making coffee, he heard voices singing along to 'Thoroughly Modern Millie' and a few steps of a Charleston thumping on the floor. Evelyn shouted directions over the music.

'No. It's step-ball-change step-ball-change *then* the Suzie-Qs in a square!'

He suspected that he had invited them so as to force a stamp of finality on his decision. With no witnesses, he would have been able to relinquish his parenthood to Henry's jealousy and the machinations of the DHSS; now that he was socially and emotionally a father, the official part was reduced in effect to the thinnest of red tape. He had often harboured doubts as to whether Henry actually liked telling him what to do. Perhaps if he challenged her rule by standing on his own two feet for once, he would earn her respect and regain her love. She always scoffed at the mention of 'settling down', so by presenting Dad with a grandchild he was doing her a favour. Encouraged by Marie-Claude, Dad would find the whole affair uproariously funny, of course. As Evelyn said, once Hilary made it clear he was to drop teaching in favour of fatherhood, he would give the venture full financial support. At the final reckoning, Dad was more childish than any of them; a regular flow of cash had kept maturity ever at bay.

In the living room, Julie Andrews was discarded in favour of some Shirley Bassey religious kitsch. The percolator gargled fragrantly. Hilary stacked cups on a tray and unwrapped a box of chocolates that Debbie had brought along instead of wine. And Rufus?

Through the half-open door, he saw Richard cross himself and fall on his knees,

'Fruc-ta ven-tris too-ooo-ees,' sang Richard, pointing to the bathroom where the baby lay. As the 'Slumbersoftie Man' himself had pointed out earlier this evening, Hilary had given Rufus a badly needed emotional/moral slap by finally playing the turning worm. As Evelyn had pointed out, Rufus, like teaching English, was one of the things Hilary was allowing to clog up the path to freedom out of sheer force of habit. As Debbie, whose sister had conceived through the obliging agency of a gay boy friend, pointed out, children won hands down over men because they *had* to stay with you for at least sixteen years, after which time you could be sure they would never get you from under their skin. Hilary pressed a chocolate against the roof of his mouth with his tongue and sensed that they were right, all three. He was well-rid of a lover who was a walking mockery to the name and who brought him nothing but insecurity. Free of Rufus and teaching, he would enter a new phase of self-development. To give Daniel a happy home he had to be fulfilled in other realms than fatherhood, so he would divide his time between baby and career. As soon as he was old enough for the crêche at the dance studios, Dan could crawl around there with the other orphans of Terpsichore, while Daddy regained his former steel-edged technique and flung himself back into auditions. He would audition for straight plays, too, since twenty-five was a trifle old for a chorus boy. While child and parent glowed with felicitous vitality, Rufus could plough right on with the one-night-stands and piano lessons, and stew in his own dreariness.

Hilary almost dropped the trayful of percolator and chocolates, for Rufus was standing on the opposite pavement, staring up at the living-room window. He had no umbrella against the driving rain and his hair was flattened. As he moved a few feet into the beam of light thrown out between the curtains, Hilary noticed a pronounced limp. He clanked the tray to the floor and thrust up the landing window.

'Rufus! Hi!' he called. His throat was dry with wine and it was a strain to project his voice. Raindrops stung his cheeks as he leaned further out. He couldn't see Rufus' expression. Perhaps it wasn't Rufus? What the hell? 'Wait a second, I'm coming right down.'

He pulled the window down again with a force that sent paint splinters over the carpet. As he crossed the landing a pitiful wail arose in the bathroom. He started down the stairs but was checked by the cry. Drawn back, he ran into the darkened room where the cot had been dragged and snatched Daniel out of the bedding. He remembered that Rufus didn't know about Dan. No more doorway shocks.

'Brij,' he shouted, causing Dan to bellow. 'Bridget!' Shirley Bassey was too loud. He ran into the room. 'Brij, could you hold him a sec? He's fed up and Rufus is at the door.'

'What?' shrieked Bridget, smiling. Richard thought they had come in to play and took Dan's little hands in a parody of the Twist. Vowing he would never treat his child like a parcel again, Hilary thrust Dan into the nearest unpractised grip and sprinted down the stairs.

Coats had fallen off their hooks and were blocking the door. He hurled them out of his path and tugged his way to the street. Rufus had moved. Hilary glanced along one way, then the other. Rufus had vanished. Putting the lock on 'latch', he pulled the door to and ran across the road to the nearest pub. Assailed by sudden noise and lights and the stench of smoke and spilt bitter, he walked rapidly across the saloon, trawling the crowd with his gaze. Hopeless. He drifted panting back to the flat.

A boy scampered along the pavement, mimicking an ambulance siren as he went. He was scraping what looked like a windscreen wiper along the complaining brickwork.

Richard met Hilary in the hall and hugged him. Patting his damp back he murmured kindly,

'Come on, Daddy, come along. Just a vile dream.'

119

# Chapter Twenty-Two

Henry picked up the wrapper of the chocolate digestives she had devoured in last night's nervous fury. Smiling to herself, she tossed it into the bin. She poured a glass of grapefruit juice and glanced at her watch; it was absurdly late. If missing the start of morning surgery felt so good, she would try it more often. The imprudent lack of sleep heightened her exhilaration. She took a sip of juice to knock back her vitamin tablets, then tiptoed to the bed, crouching to kiss a handful of toes before guiding a straying foot back beneath the duvet.

An anaemic sun lit a landscape hard with frost. The bitter chill had descended with the last of the rain five or more hours ago. The roads would be a skating rink. He mumbled something incomprehensible and nuzzled deeper into his clutch of pillows.

On her return from Walpole Tower she had staggered in, downed a tumblerful of Scotch and collapsed in the armchair with a refill in her hand, the packet of chocolate digestives on her lap and a heartful of renewed anger at Andrew's childish behaviour. She wolfed several biscuits in fast succession, rang Marie-Claude, spoke to Dad's answering machine, and had fallen heavily asleep half-way through her third fat Scotch and a radio discussion of the psychological necessity of urban green space.

She had woken from a spirit-and-sugar-drugged doze some time after midnight, hearing the door buzzer insistently sounded. Still drunk, barely conscious, she had released the entry-phone lock and admitted a dripping, near-hysterical man who claimed to have been mugged by seven lesbian gypsies. As she sat in the armchair trying to focus, Andrew had cried apologies for a while, clutching her astonished knees. Then he had proceeded to explain that he had misled her with silence and actually was nothing more top secret than a piano teacher. Furthermore, he went on to confess, he was not, nor had he ever been, married. There was a fiancée of sorts, he said, but he had taken the liberty of breaking off with her for the sake of Sandy. Henry had asked who Sandy was. He looked up nonplussed, whereupon she had seen her mistake, shrugged her shoulders and heard herself launch into an improbable relation of how in real life she was a high-powered psychiatrist but that men were always scared off by this so she was forced to pose as something more erotic and less awe-inspiring. Oh yes, and her real name was Henrietta, but her friends called her Henry, her mother was dead and her father remarried and living in France. There was also a younger brother called Hilary who taught English. For some reason this had prompted a renewed tide of wordless lamentation on his part which she had stemmed in the first and most natural way that came to mind.

As she burrowed in her desk for pen and paper, Henry recalled with fresh delight that it had been like making love with a quite different person – which, in a sense, he had been. Less overwhelming, perhaps, but sweetly reassuring and infinitely easier to live with. Did she say *live*?

Unable to find a pen, she took a much chewed pencil and sharpened it with the bread knife. Then she gulped the rest of the fruit juice, consulting as she did so a letter with a French postmark. She sucked the tip of the pencil briefly, reaching for inspiration, then wrote.

Darling Rufus, (A *much* sexier name than Andrew. So glad)
    Have had to race off to work. Coffee, fruit juice, bread etcetera on worktop. Help yourself. Ditto bath, telephone, radio etcetera.

She hesitated, chewed the pencil for a second, then continued.

    Spare keys on hook behind bathroom door.
    Now listen. Have just got letter inviting me for interview at amazing new *institut psychologique* at Fontainebleau on Tuesday. Intend taking long weekend to stay with parents in Paris

beforehand. They invite you, I merely demand. Forget ferry cost as I claim it back on expenses. Pack your bags. Night boat leaves Dover at 11.30.

Having thought up lots of good reasons why you can't possibly come, forget them, ring the number I have circled above and say yes.

Love?
Henry.

# Chapter Twenty-Three

Sumitra waited disconsolate on *Shri Metcalfe*'s sofa. From downstairs came the excited chatter of *Ba*, Kamala and several women neighbours. His flat was silent save for the electronically simulated tick of his alarm clock to her right. Dan's cot lay empty, but the paraphernalia that had become his was still scattered about the room. Sumitra had picked up a teddy which used to be hers; it was a dusty pink with a black leather nose and one eye was mising. She dangled the creature absently by a suedette paw.

She had skipped the last period of the afternoon. It was English with her lord and master, so by rights she should have been there, but Kerry and Tamsin had made her life a misery so she had run away home. They had crept up on her when she was at her devotions and seen inside her locker. Though Kerry had tried to hold her down, she had fought like a tigress and managed somehow to padlock the door again. They had trailed her nonetheless all afternoon, jeering, parodying her father's bubbling accent.

'Oh my golly gosh, I am so very much in love with Mister Metcalfe,' Tamsin kept shouting, rolling her eyes and holding her palms together.

Sumitra had dawdled on the short journey back home so as to quell her mother's doubts. *Ba* held a strict regard for punctuality and her views on truancy were severe. Despite her daughter's trip around the block and in and out of the mobile library, her suspicions were aroused. No sooner had she begun her inquisition, however, when the doorbell rang and Kamala walked in with a handsome white man. They were both in expensive leather jackets. *Ba* had stood astonished, wiping her hands on her plastic apron. Kamala had stood on the threshold, all solemn, and said, 'Hello, *Ba*. This is Brian, my husband. I thought it was time you all met.'

Then *Ba* had greeted them both just as solemnly, like strangers, and gestured for them to walk into the sitting room. She shut the door on them, then raised a finger to Sumitra and snapped, 'Not a word from you, layabout. Get upstairs to *Shri Metcalfe*'s flat and watch the baby for me. And send in your *Baba* from the shop.'

Sumitra had done as she was bidden, and spent a happy ten minutes cooing over the Holy Child and walking around *Shri Metcalfe*'s rooms, touching his private clothes, looking at his pictures and thumbing through his glamorous record collection. Startled from this idyll by banging on the door, she had scampered down to the hall, enjoying the charade of 'mistress of the house' and assuming that her lord and master had forgotten his key.

It wasn't him. Two burly types were standing there with an empty carrycot and one of them asked, 'Mr Metcalfe in then, lovey?'

'No,' she mumbled, starting to shut the door on them as she had seen *Ba* do. 'He's still at school. He's teaching.'

They pushed past her however and started up the stairs.

'That's all right. He sent for us,' said the one who hadn't spoken.

Sure that this was all wrong, somehow, she had chased them upstairs just in time to see the bigger of the two slinging a loudly protesting Dan into their carrycot. She ran at him and attempted to tug the handles from his grasp, but his henchman swung her bodily off the ground and sat her firmly on the sofa. One vast, bristle-backed hand restrained the frantic efforts of her two small scratching ones.

'You stay there like a good little darlin',' he said, 'and when His Nibs gets in, give him this form. It's so he can reclaim expenses.'

'Cheerio,' said the other. Then they had taken Dan and left.

The whole episode had lasted barely three minutes and she had not moved since, save to pick up the teddy. Downstairs her father was striking a business bargain with his new son-in-law

124

while the women – exclaiming the while – flicked through brochures for kitchen units and holidays in the sun. Downstairs there came the familiar jangle of *Shri Metcalfe*'s bicycle mounting the pavement and the clatter of his key in the lock. Sumitra frowned and swung the teddy slightly.

# Chapter Twenty-Four

Not a good day. He had been cruelly over-hung, gulping fresh air and vitamin C at every possible interval. A glass of wine at lunchtime for a fellow teacher's birthday had helped matters briefly, but had left him perilously somnolent all afternoon. The senior English class had been spectacularly unfair, asking impossible questions like why is *A Winter's Tale* so boring and why couldn't they analyse American soap opera instead? A session with 15B had followed, from which little Sumitra Sharma had fled as he arrived, in floods of tears. He had rounded on the more spiteful little white girls there and accused them of teasing her. An ugly scene had ensued, culminating in a disciplinary on-the-spot grammar quiz, which he would now have to mark along with a thickish block of commentaries on the least-favourite poem by his least-favourite Lake poet.

Once outside school grounds, however, his spirits had begun to lift. There was his new-found freedom to consider. He had thought of handing in his notice in person today, but had shelved this plan in favour of a carefully worded letter next week; he could never tell when a reference might be needed and therefore wanted to tread on as few administrative corns as possible. He would feed Dan, bathe them both, then sit in a studious heap. Perhaps if he penned the resignation letter first, the marking would seem less of a labour. He stopped off at the newsagents on the corner to buy his first copy of *The Stage* in months. It bore the good news that a Croydon theatre was holding auditions for a new production of *Kismet*, with the distinct possibility of a West End transfer.

Remounting his bicycle, he saw Evelyn's torn-off windscreen wiper lying in the gutter, remembered last night, then suppressed the memory as quickly as he had conjured it.

A flashy new car was parked outside the Sharmas' shop; a yellow one with teeth and eyelids. Bharat Sharma was not serving – which was strange – and judging from the noise coming through the hall wall, his wife was throwing a party, which was stranger still. He wheeled his bike to its resting place in the hall, kicked the front door shut and went up. It was very quiet upstairs. He wondered how long Shanti Sharma had left Dan unattended, then was startled to find her little daughter waiting for him. Sumitra jumped up from the sofa, dropping Dan's teddy as she did so. Her face glistened with tears.

'Hello, *Shri Metcalfe*,' she said.

'Hello,' he replied, crouching slightly. 'Why weren't you in class? Whatever's the matter?' He smiled, but she glanced away. 'Sumitra, what's wrong?' He made as if to approach her but she ran to the cot and, before he could stop her, tugged it off balance and on to the floor. The effort caused her to grunt. A felt ball with a bell inside it rolled jangling out of the empty bedding.

'They came and took him away!' she shouted. 'Your horrid men came and took him in a plastic bag with handles.'

'Which men?'

'There were two. One was very fat. They said you'd sent them and it was all right.'

Finally she started to cry in earnest, in hard, wrenched little sobs. She stood with the crook of one arm across her eyes and her small frame shook.

'There. Ssh. It's not your fault,' Hilary started to say, but she ran stamping past him and down the stairs. He heard the front door open, then slam behind her.

He set the cot upright once more, then walked around the room making a stack in his arms; changing mat, anorak, clean baby-gro, teddy, pack of nappies. He piled them all up in the bucket, which he nestled on top of the cot. Gingerly, because it was hard to see where he was going, he carried the lot down to the hall for Mrs Sharma to collect when she had time.

The answering machine had recorded five messages in his absence. On his return to the living room he pressed 'play', then lay on the sofa-bed staring at the ceiling as he listened.

'Hello, Hil. It's Evelyn. Thanks so very much for a lovely party last night. Dan's quite enchanting and I'd be delighted to godmother him for you. I bumped into Hannah – Hannah Flowers – in the library this morning and mentioned the possible court case and she'd be delighted to help out. She'd like to meet you in any case. Anyway, lovely party. 'Bye.'

'Hi, Possum. It's Brij,' said Bridget. 'Blissy evening and even blissier baby. *What* a clever boy you are! Many thanks. Let's go and get legless soon. Oh, and I've found a marvellous black babysitter for you. *A bientôt.*'

'Hello, Hilary. It's Henry here. Look, I've been asked for an interview at the new research hospital at Fontainebleau, so I'm off to stay with Dad and M–C tonight. Back next week sometime. Thursday or Wednesday probably. If you ring me before I go and let me know what they gave you, I'll thank them for you. Otherwise I'll just send love. Oh God. I've still got your present by the bread-bin, haven't I? Come to supper when I get back so you can pick it up. Ring me, anyway. 'Bye.'

'Hilary Metcalfe? This is Peter Gorbling at the Department of Health and Social Security. We would like to make certain inquiries regarding your domestic situation.' There was a pause, then a gale of laughter. 'Had you fooled, didn't I?' said Richard. 'Bravo! You've been and gone and done it now. We're all very proud. No, honestly. Get Brij or someone to babysit and we can go dancing later on. There's something going on at Helen's, I think. I'm out now – auditions for Dutch lager; not me I know but *il faut souffrir pour le cash*. Back sevenish, but the machine's on so you could always chat to that. T'ra.'

'Hi, Hil. It's big sister again. Sorry. I forgot to mention. There was some problem with picking up that blasted baby, but I spoke to the DHSS woman and she said she'd get someone round there today. 'Spect Mrs Wotsit will let them in for you. Lots of love.'

The machine stopped, bleeped and rewound its tape.

Hilary drifted through to the kitchen to pour himself a glass of coke. The feeding bottle lay on top of the fridge. He started to put it away, then slumped against a wall, pressed the bottle to his baking forehead and, doubling up, wept.

128

He wanted his mother, but his mother was his sister and she was going to France. He slid on to a chair, still clutching the bottle, and tried to tug off a piece of kitchen towel. He had no hand free to steady the roll, however, and the thing fell, unfurling, to the floor. Sobbing, nose bubbling, lips swollen, he clambered after it and almost laughed. Gasping for breath more steadily, he went back to pouring himself a coke and put the feeding bottle back inside the fridge.

The drink calmed him. He was hung-over, that was half the problem. Fresh air always helped. He would take a smallish ride before it got dark and when he got back he could pour himself a proper drink and start ringing people up. It was Friday night, after all. Richard could take him dancing again, or to Helen's if it was a party. The marking would have to wait.

He hadn't used his Walkman that morning because his head had been throbbing. He took it now, slipped the headphones over his ears, pressed the play button and set out. A late afternoon sun was out and Mary Martin gave him her vehement assurance:

'I expect every one
Of my crowd to make fun
Of my proud protestations
Of faith in romance.'

Hil sang along with the thundering string punctuation, making a noise like a tuba. Sumitra was skipping on the pavement with a little boy. He waved to them and pedalled towards the Wood Lane junction.

'And you'll say I'm naive
As a babe to believe
Any fable I hear
From a person in pants!'

Somewhere in the background a lorry sounded its horn.

# Chapter Twenty-Five

He had posed as the *Narendra Saraswati* and been found out.
Her respectful devotion to him was now passion for an heroic
trickster, and she waited gloomily for the punishment that
must surely be meted out. After bathing her eyes at the kitchen
sink, she slipped through the chattering women to the privacy
of her own room. Here she silently let fly. She cracked the
stolen record with her shoe and cut the palm of each hand with
one of the fragments. Wincing, she hid the wounds with
sticking plaster and ran back out to the street. If questioned,
she would tell them she had fallen over.

A small boy was dragging a skipping-rope past the shop-
front.

'Let me show you how,' she said.

He passed it to her, brightening. Deftly she whirled the rope
about her and skipped, staring hard at the passing cars to
concentrate her important thoughts.

'All in together, girls,' sang the boy and clapped in time with
her thumping sandals. 'Never mind the weather, girls. When it
is your birthday, please jump OUT!'

As panic hardened into deadly calm, there crystalized the
resolve that when *Shri Metcalfe*'s moment came, she would
have to die with him as a would-be propagator of a false
religion.

'January. February. March. April.'

He might at least gain some consolation from her puny
solidarity. She skipped faster, hurrying the boy's recitation of
months, then saw *Shri Metcalfe* leaving the flat. He rode past
and waved; she stopped skipping and forgot to smile back.

130

The boy chased the bike and on impulse she chased the boy, letting fall the skipping-rope in her haste. She saw him cross Wood Lane on his bicycle and froze.

She saw the lorry as it bore down on him from the left, but she couldn't shout. The lorry hooted twice, then pulled on its brakes with a screech as he rode into its path. The little boy laughed, turning to Sumitra for approval. *Shri Metcalfe* almost escaped, but the lorry struck his rear wheel and as the bicycle was torn beneath the giant tyres, he was flung up to where the lorry's radiator smote him squarely on the back. His body was whipped in a broken heap to the side of the road.

As the ensemble of horns burst out in the queue behind the lorry, Sumitra sensed that she was not allowed to die quite yet, being ordained for a secondary purpose. Leaving the boy to stare, she ran to the kiosk on a nearby corner and summoned an ambulance. Then she pushed through the gathering crowd and cast herself weeping on to his body. Huge white hands tried to haul her off, but she cried the louder. All she could think was that suddenly she was closer to *Shri Metcalfe* than she had ever been or was likely to be again. There was a thick streak of blood running from under his hair, and his legs were twisted unnaturally.

'Don't touch me. I love him,' she announced and the hands let her alone. A woman thrust her head against his chest and announced that there were still signs of life.

'Come on, dearie,' said a black man in a uniform. 'Is he your Dad? Where do you live, then?'

'I love him,' she informed him.

'Have you ever been in an ambulance?' he asked.

'No. I won't leave him.'

'He's coming too.'

The ambulance was quiet as night inside. A cheerful woman with white hair tied *Shri Metcalfe* to a bed and held a plastic mask over his face. The mask hissed.

'Are you gassing him?' Sumitra asked.

'No, love. This is to keep him alive.'

'Oh, good.'

Could this be a reprieve? Sumitra crouched on the floor of the ambulance and held one of his lovely hands to her lips and cheek, feeling the long bones in the fingers.

'Who's a good girl!' said the woman with the white hair.
'What do you know?' thought Sumitra and gave her her briefest smile.

# Chapter Twenty-Six

Thoroughly in control of last night's sentimental pilgrimage, which he now dismissed as mere biological function, Rufus stepped out of the taxi at North Pole Road ready to explain all. He paid the driver with some of the money he had found in Henrietta's kitchen drawer and rang her brother's doorbell. For the first time in his life, truth seemed to be on his side. Last night he had confessed almost everything to 'Sandy', fearing the worst reaction, and had prompted a startling confession in return. Now he would make a clean breast of everything to Hilary. He was less sure how to tackle the problem of having effectively run off with the sister-in-law. In the extremity of the previous night, her revelation had struck him a blow from which he reeled afresh on waking. He had always known that Hilary had a sister called Henrietta, and what she did, but Hilary had cherished some idea that she disapproved of his lifestyle and so had kept the two of them apart. The only relative he had met had been that elderly, Volvo-driving godmother. Given that Henrietta had lied – well, that they had both lied – the misunderstanding was quite explicable. Given Hilary and Henrietta's strong physical resemblance, the sexual attraction was perfectly straightforward. He would feed the final, delicate gobbets of truth to her while they were in France.

No one came to the door. Denying that he felt remotely furtive, Rufus fished out his key and let himself in. He would make some tea, give Hilary half an hour to come back from wherever he was, then he would leave a charming letter (and possibly the key) before travelling home to pack his things.

The hall was almost blocked by a baby's cot filled with

nappies and things. Presumably the vestiges of Mrs Sharma's niece or whatever she had been. He climbed the stairs, conscious of a faint, medicinal smell that was not normally there. A boxful of empty wine bottles was waiting on the landing. Three full ashtrays lay on the kitchen table and what looked like a case of port lay on the lino underneath it. Rufus put the kettle on to boil and sat down. His heart leapt as he saw a pamphlet about DHSS tribunals. He frowned, as Hilary wasn't signing on so far as he knew.

The day's moral courage was still strong and he hoped Hilary would come home soon. A letter was shamefaced and emotionally unfinished; he needed to suffer as some kind of expiation. A radio was playing in the Sharmas' flat below; the kind of music Rufus abhorred. He pulled out the newspaper he was sitting on. It was a copy of *The Stage* and a bold red ring had been drawn around the announcement of an audition for chorus (male) for a revival of *Kismet* in Croydon. Same old hopeful Hil! The kettle came noisily to the boil and Rufus stood to turn it off. He opened the fridge. The only milk was inside a baby's bottle and he took out the incongruous article between finger and thumb – doubtless some joke of Richard's. The fluid looked watery. He unscrewed the teat and sniffed; the bottle had been washed in something medicinal. He wrinkled his nose and poured some of its contents into a mug. Staring at the dusk falling outside, he saw one of the yellow street-lamps flicker to life and knew that he was the proverbial heel. He determined to write a letter now and run away. If he saw the boy face to face, he'd have to stay. He'd be caught. Forgetting tea, panicking almost, he tore a sheet off the notepad on the wall and was looking for a pen when the telephone rang. He answered it without thinking.

'Hello?'

'Is that Hilary Metcalfe's house?'

'It is.'

'It's Hammersmith Hospital here. We wanted to contact his family.'

'What's happened to him?' asked Rufus, feeling sick.

'Sorry. Who am I speaking to?'

'A friend. We live together. What's happened?'

'There was an accident. He's in a serious condition, but we

think he'll be all right.'

'You must ring his sister.' Rufus felt a burning in the pit of his chest. 'She's his only kin in the country. Dr Henrietta Metcalfe at Princess Marina's Hospital.'

'Ah yes. We've got that number here. And could I have your name please, Sir?'

'Andrew. No. I mean . . . Oh fuck!'

Rufus dropped the receiver. Within seconds he was down the stairs, out of the door and running down the road to his lover.

# Chapter Twenty-Seven

'Bloody hell,' shouted Henry, honking her horn at some pedestrians as she pulled off the Westway like a demon. Through waiting for them to cross, she was forced to stop at a red light. Flashes of hatred at Hilary for raining on her parade before it had even set out alternated with hasty oblations of superstitious apology: 'Don't go and die. Oh, God. Please no,' she muttered. The light changed and she swerved off to the left in hot pursuit of Hammersmith Hospital.

Buoyed up by the tandem treats of being invited to the Fontainebleau institute and learning that Rufus, unlike the late Andrew, was an eligible bachelor, she had floated through work. The telephone had rung half-way through the last consultation of the afternoon. Just half an hour before the latter started, Rufus had called to deliver a definite yes, so she had been lending only half an ear to old Ewan Cockburn and his dreary anal-oriented fantasies, working out how long she had to pack, run a check on the car and knock up something for them to eat. Then the bleak message had come through from the hospital.

She knew that they never announced sudden deaths over the telephone, in case the newly bereaved drove badly and caused further casualties, but she drove like a maniac in any case, convinced that he was going to die before she could reach his side. She winced as she caught herself planning how best to postpone the interview in France without jeopardizing her chances.

'I'm Dr Metcalfe. My brother's just been admitted to Intensive Care. Which way is it?' she asked, terrified of being shepherded into one of the small pink rooms they reserved for the breaking of bad news. There was one at Princess Marina's; it had boxes of tissues, a kettle, sugar lumps and some teabags. She crossed her fingers behind her back.

'Hello, Doctor,' said the nurse. 'I'll show you the way. Sister Fraser, could you hold the fort?'

Henry followed her sensible shoes down two corridors, her fingers slowly unclenching. She explained to the nurse that she was a big, brave doctor and would like the bad news now rather than later.

'He's unconscious,' said the nurse, 'but breathing fine. His legs are in a bad way, but nothing time won't mend. The concussion is pretty severe.'

'Did he fracture his skull?' Henry asked, keeping her voice professionally steady.

'I'm afraid so.'

'Poor chap,' Henry muttered. She had fleeting visions: Hilary with a stroke; Hilary unable to eat properly; Hilary with a lopsided smile; Hilary unable to walk without a built-up shoe; Hilary – oh Christ – unable to dance. The nurse stopped at a door.

'Here we are,' she said brightly. 'Unit Fourteen. I'll be back at the desk if you need anything. I'll send Dr Palmer round to chat with you?'

'Bill Palmer?'

'That's right.'

'Thanks.'

'Your brother's young friend and daughter are in there with him.'

'What?' Henry paused with her hand on the door and felt a wave of relief. 'Then there must have been some mistake. His name's Hilary Metcalfe and he's twenty-five.'

The nurse's brow furrowed as she checked a card on a board by the door.

'Yes,' she said. 'It's definitely him.'

Henry peered through the window into Intensive Care, Unit Fourteen. 'Oh I see,' she said, seeing. 'Thanks.'

The nurse said not at all and walked back to her post. Henry remained where she was for a moment to muster some measure of control.

His 'daughter', evidently some administrative misunderstanding as she was the daughter of his Asian landlords, sat in a chair by one wall, staring lugubriously at his bed. His 'young friend' sat close by, holding one of his hands in his.

'Damn. Damn. *Shit*,' said Henry slowly, then took a breath and stepped inside.

Rufus rose at once. She had been worrying about what to say, but he came straight over and took her in his arms. He hugged her warmly, his cheek wet on her neck.

'Hi,' he mumbled into her jersey and gave a fruity sniff. She stared over his shoulder at the little girl.

'Hello,' she said to him. 'It was kind of you to come.'

'I love him,' the girl declared and returned her gaze to the bed.

'It's all rather hard to explain,' Rufus began, still into her jersey.

'But he was your fiancée?' she finished for him.

Rufus gave her another hug as answer. He sighed. No, he didn't. Hilary sighed. Simultaneously they raised their heads and looked at the bed where her brother lay. His head was fetchingly bound in spotless white. The sheet was lifted off his legs by a wire cage. A monitor was wired into one of the pillows. She took the nearest hand and pressed it, making a mental note to bring him in some decent pyjamas.

'Hil? It's Henry. Henry and . . . Henry and Rufus. You're going to be OK.'

'Yes,' added Rufus, rubbing the other hand.

'What the fuck were you two doing, behaving like that at my deathbed?' Hilary asked from behind his bandages.

'Thank God. He's going to be all right. He's trying to say something,' said his sister, relief chasing urgency across her face. Behind them the little Asian girl slipped out unnoticed.

'I suppose that this is the moment for me to treat you to my acclaimed rendition of "Hello, Young Lovers",' continued Hilary.

'Yes, he's really trying,' said Rufus. 'Shall I fetch a doctor?'

# Chapter Twenty-Eight

Holding her torch in one hand and the can of lighter fuel in the other, Sumitra anointed first the photograph from Starbright Agency, then liberally doused the rest of the shrine. From a paper bag she produced the fragments of the record destroyed in holy wrath that afternoon, and heaped them into the votive saucer together with the DHSS expenses claim form. She added some Dolly Mixture for old time's sake and then, mimicking the criminals she had seen in films, she squirted the fluid down the front of the locker and along the floor in a trail to the door. Carefully she closed the tunnel, and wrapped the tin back in its newspaper covering. She pushed the whole into one of her raincoat pockets, then wiped her hands spotlessly clean on a handkerchief which had once blown off his washing line. It said 'H' on one corner in red embroidery. It was very precious, but her present joy was worth any sacrifice.

Her tongue protruding with concentration, she crouched and pressed the square of linen on to the tail end of the lighter fuel trail. Hands on the ground before her, so that there was a pleasing twinge from her bandaged wounds of love, she lowered her head and kissed the relic farewell.

Away in a classroom to her right, a cuckoo clock struck midnight. Sumitra shivered. A frost sparkled on the play-ground tarmac and beneath her raincoat she had on only a nightdress for warmth. She rose from her pose of humble thanks and produced a box of matches from her pocket. With one neat gesture she struck one and let it fall, burning, to the soaking linen.

The flame spread along the trail with a sound like a short

puff of breath. The shrine ignited with something like a cough and sent a satisfying bouquet of little flame sprays out onto the lockers around it.

Sumitra clapped her hands for pure delight and, eyes wide, began to sing,

'Getting to know you,
Getting to know all about you.'

Pulling her raincoat about her, she scampered out to the playground.

'Getting to like you,
Getting to hope you like me.'

Through the windows, she could make out the whiteish gold of the growing pyre.

'Haven't you noticed? Suddenly I'm free and easy
Because of all the wonderful and new
Things I'm learning about you . . .'

Hilary would live. She was in love. The cold bit at her calves on the way home, but still she lingered a while to dance.